HARD PLASTIC DOLLS

by Polly and Pam Judd

Published by  Hobby House Press, Inc.

Cumberland, MD 2150'

ACKNOWLEDGEMENTS

There have been many people who have helped the authors in the completion of this book. We would like to take this opportunity to acknowledge and thank them for their help.

We would especially like to thank The Cleveland Doll Club members for their knowledge, support and use of their dolls.

There were several individuals who helped in various sections of the book. Pat Parton aided in the development of the identification guide. Marianne Gardner provided information about the Nancy Ann Storybook Dolls and dolls by Madame Alexander.

The catalog material for the Ideal section of the book was furnished by Joanne Calhoun of CBS Toys.

There were many people who permitted us to use their dolls in the photographs or helped us in other ways. They include: Pat Parton, Mary Ann Gardner, Sandy Strater, Rosemary Romance, Barbara Comienski, Nancy Roeder, Laura Brown, Beatrice Campbell, Marie Ezzo, Lois Seketa, Helen Krielow, Anita Philpott, Jackie Kaner, Thelma Purvis, Louise Schnell, Aunt Onie, Ruth Glover, Wanda Lodwick, Phyllis Appell, Gail Anderson, Margaret Mandel, Mary Jane Poley, Lillian Sakal, Mel Appell, Mary Beth Manchook, Emily MacCord, Heloise Miles, Helen Kirschnick, Dolly Jakubecz, Anna Barile, Ann Lotterman, Barbara Church, Jane Gage, Jean Canaday, Mary Lou Trowbridge, Sophie Zeman, Ursula Schink, Kathy Zimmermann, Cindy Bezdek, John Ezzo, Ann Pendleton and Mavis Mohr.

We also wish to thank our editor, Donna H. Felger, and the entire staff of Hobby House Press, Inc.

Finally, we would like to thank Wallace Judd, husband and father, who has been very patient and supportive.

Additional Copies of this book may be purchased at $12.95
from
HOBBY HOUSE PRESS, INC.
900 Frederick Street
Cumberland, Maryland 21502
or from your favorite bookstore or dealer.
Please add $1.75 per copy postage.

Third Printing, August 1988
Second Printing, January 1987
© 1985 Polly and Pam Judd

TABLE OF CONTENTS

PREFACE

Every doll collection has a "beginning." For us, it was the opening of a Goodwill store in our community, and the discovery of a beautiful bride doll unstrung in an old shoe box. The letters "A.C." on the back of the head were mysterious and challenging. The doll's body material was strange, shiny and beautiful. We were captivated.

Many years, many dolls and many reference books later, we learned that the bride was an American Character doll, and she had been manufactured in the early 1950s. She was hard plastic.

Although our collection is eclectic, we both find ourselves drawn to these beautiful, durable dolls. We realize that collectors today are seriously selecting these dolls for investment as well as beauty. However, after hours of research, we have learned that their identification is still difficult. This is especially true because so many of these dolls are completely unmarked.

Many doll writers have included this type of doll in their books. They have published pictures helpful in identification. Magazines have published some articles about a few of the hard plastic types. However, the information is scattered and often unavailable when needed. Also, many of these dolls still remain relatively unknown.

While it is not possible to have all the information in one short book, we felt that a small paperback handbook that could easily be carried should be written about hard plastic dolls, marked and unmarked.

The book should list various doll companies and the dolls they produced. It should show typical pictures of the dolls of these companies. It should show typical pictures of the dolls of these companies with current prices.

There should also be an identification guide for unmarked dolls or those with obscure marks. This book, with its price guide, could be easily carried to doll shows, flea markets, antique stores as well as used at home.

Dolls included in this book are:
1. All hard plastic.
2. Dolls with vinyl heads and hard plastic bodies.
3. Baby dolls with hard plastic heads and cloth, latex and rubber bodies.

In working with the information available, and in looking at hundreds of dolls, we find that hard plastic identification is usually easier than with other types of dolls. The production period is short (1946 to 1959), and relatively few large companies produced the dolls.

INTRODUCTION TO HARD PLASTIC DOLLS

The beautiful hard plastic dolls appeared on the market after World War II. They were eagerly purchased by parents and friends of the war babies who had grown up with the meager offerings of a wartime economy.

They were made of a new material which had been perfected for war use. They were durable. They looked like the composition dolls so beloved before the hostilities. They could be made similar to the old composition, and thus they were available quickly. But most of all, they reflected the traditional American beauty so desired by a post war generation.

Such existing manufacturers as American Character, Arranbee, Alexander, Effanbee, Horsman, Nancy Ann Storybook Dolls and Vogue vied with each other to add the new hard plastic lines to their dwindling stocks of composition dolls. Often they used up odd assortments of heads, limbs and bodies in the rush to get them to market, and these early dolls sometimes had unusual mixtures of body parts.

New manufacturers such as Terri Lee and the Duchess Doll Corp. joined in competing for the market. Each tried new combinations of plastics and claimed that theirs was the best.

Henry DuBois in his book, *Plastic History of the U.S.A.*, credits Horsman Dolls with introducing the plastisol doll in 1946 although Latexture Products produced a mannequin doll during the war which they said was made of a "plastic material."

Violet Grandwold used the new material also in 1946 and introduced the *Terri Lee* family. This added a new dimension into costuming for dolls. Little girls clamored for both the dolls and their costumes.

Effanbee quickly followed with *Li'l Darling* in 1947 and *Honey Ballerina* in 1948.

Also in 1948 A & H made a 7in (17.8cm) *Lady Hamilton* inexpensive doll which was a forerunner of the fancy dolls which graced the shelves of a little girl's room rather than her toy chest. Millions of these hard plastic adult-type fashion dolls were manufactured in the next few years.

In 1948, the Ideal Novelty and Toy Company created the popular *Toni* doll which advertised the home permanent hair styling kits manufactured by The Toni Company. Sears Roebuck & Co. was one of the major distributors of these all-hard plastic dolls whose hair could be washed and set. The *Toni* doll came in various sizes, hair colors and costumes.

Madame Alexander changed doll history and doll collecting in 1948 when she introduced the hard plastic *Little Women* dolls. This was the beginning of a line of dolls that are the most coveted hard plastic dolls in the eyes of collectors today. She quickly followed up with *Babs*, the *Ice Skater, Nina Ballerina* and *Alice in Wonderland* in 1949.

While many companies marked their dolls, many of the others produced totally unmarked dolls. To further confuse identification, most of the manufacturers made unmarked dolls from the same line for Sears and Montgomery Ward and other mail order houses. Department stores would order special editions, and these, too, were both marked and unmarked.

During the first several years after World War II, in the rush to get dolls into production, companies would share factories and assembly lines, and odd combinations of dolls appeared. Throughout the period, companies would share molds, especially for body parts. They even shared marks at times.

Today doll collectors treasure the dolls of this era. Sadly, the days of the hard plastic dolls were numbered. New inventions such as vinyl made them obsolete by the mid-1950s. (A major exception is the Alexander Doll Company which still produces a type of hard plastic dolls.) Then rooted hair, implanted in the soft vinyl, was a key change in the structure of the hard plastic dolls.

Lucky were the collectors who prized the early Alexanders, *Tonis*, Eugenias, *Betsy McCalls* and *Ginnys*. In the past 30 years, they have become highly collectible, and each year they seem to be more expensive and difficult to obtain.

Happily for the collector, these dolls seem to be among the least destructible ever made. They do not break like china and bisque dolls. They do not craze like the compositions or powder like the vinyls.

DIFFERENCES AMONG HARD PLASTIC, COMPOSITION AND VINYL DOLLS

In trying to identify hard plastic dolls, it is first necessary to present information on how to differentiate these dolls from those produced directly before and after them. Generally, composition dolls came first and were followed by the total hard plastic doll. Next came a combination of a soft vinyl head on a hard plastic body, and finally vinyl dolls became standard by the late 1950s.

DIFFERENCES BETWEEN HARD PLASTIC AND COMPOSITION

Composition dolls, because they were made of paper products and glue, tend to disintegrate and/or craze as they age. This crazing is similar to that found in old, fine potteryware. The crazing takes many forms, but generally tiny cracks appear in the "skin" and get larger as the years progress. Even with seemingly smooth bodies and faces, a magnifying glass often confirms these tiny lines.

Hard plastic dolls may crack once in a while at the seams, but they do not craze, and they are extremely durable, even with hard use. If the doll is painted, the paint may chip somewhat and wear thin, especially at the head, arm and leg joints.

Hard plastic dolls usually survive changes of temperature and moisture that would disintegrate or craze the composition doll.

While both types of dolls are rigid and non-bendable to the touch except at the joints and eyes, the composition dolls tend to be and look heavier than hard plastic dolls of the same size. The details on the composition bodies such as on the feet, hands and necks are thicker. This can easily be seen. Layers of pulp materials can be observed at the head, arm and leg holes. The inside of the head, too, often shows pulp material rather than the smooth plastic.

Both types of dolls are shiny. However, the composition dolls often have a layer of an older type preservative such as varnish which can discolor and craze. This preservative has a tendency to flake and expose underlying sublayers.

DIFFERENCES BETWEEN THE HARD PLASTIC AND THE VINYL DOLL

There is a tell-tale feeling of inflexible rigidity in the hard plastic doll. Even the rigid vinyl doll is softer to the touch and will yield to firm pressure. When pressed firmly, if not careful, your fingernail can leave an impression in vinyl which is not possible in hard plastic.

While a very few of the all vinyl dolls are strung, most have jointed limbs which can be made pliable by heat and thus, inset into the doll body in place of stringing.

Most hard plastics have elastic stringing which holds the doll together. An exception to this is the hard plastic walker with a rod-like mechanism inside. This turns the head by moving the feet or vice versa. The arms are usually strung. The softer, rubber-like, more flexible vinyl does not lend itself to this type of walking apparatus. However, there are a few walking dolls from 1953 to the end of the decade that have hard plastic bodies and vinyl heads.

An easily identifiable clue to the total hard plastic identification is a wig because rooted hair came with the invention of soft vinyl. Two exceptions are the Monica dolls and a few of the American Character dolls such as *Sweet Sue, Tiny Tears* and *Betsy McCall.*

The details in the hands and feet and body of vinyl dolls are less precise, clear-cut and noticeable than the hard plastic dolls. The designers of hard plastic dolls enjoyed the artistic accuracy of the hard plastic material.

While some hard plastic was inferior and cheap in look and feel, the quality hard plastic took on some of the characteristics of a lovely bisque. It is possible for the collector today to acquire lovely quality in the less known Eugenias, Mary Hoyers, Arranbees and Nancy Anns.

Even the companies producing cheaper dolls for the mass market often produced a lovely quality plastic for a specific doll in their line. Uneeda, Eegee and Valentine were three examples.

As vinyl heads, arms and legs replaced the more rigid hard plastic, the doll designers started a trend to more realistic and less beautiful faces. The softer, more pliable vinyl allowed the whole doll to be more imaginative for children, and features were less finely molded.

Between 1957 and 1959 a change came into the quality of the hard plastic even before the advent of rigid vinyl. Such dolls as *Champagne Lady, Mother* and *Junior Miss* by Effanbee had bodies that were similar to hard plastic, but they had not reached the rigid vinyl stage of the Ideal *Miss Revlon.*

There is an artistic difference in the design of hard plastic dolls and the dolls of other eras. The war was over and people wanted to live out the dreams that had been impossible during World War II. Hard plastic girl dolls were all beautiful with regular features. Hard plastic boy dolls were all handsome. The clothes were made for parties, fashion and good times. Today we call that decade the "Fabulous Fifties."

HOW TO USE THIS BOOK

This book is set up in several ways, depending upon your knowledge of a doll. If the doll is marked and you know the company name, turn immediately to the doll company section and look up the company name which is in alphabetical order. You will find a list of dolls and their characteristics, dates of production if possible and a current price range.

If the doll is marked, but you do not know the company name (Example "R & B"), turn to the Doll Marks Section on page 258, and you will find that these letters indicate the Arranbee Company. Then turn to the Arranbee section for pictures and more references. Most marked hard plastic dolls have their numbers, letters and symbols listed in the Marks Section.

If the doll is unmarked, or if the mark is not listed, turn to the Identification Guide. There, at the beginning of the section, you will find another Table of Contents listing the various doll characteristics which will help you. Examples are eyes, mouths and walking dolls. There are many others. In this section the doll features will help you narrow the possibilities and refer you back to the doll company.

When you have exhausted these options and still have not identified your doll, return to the section, "Differences Among Hard Plastic, Composition and Vinyl Dolls." Your doll may not be hard plastic. At first it will seem difficult to tell differences in the material, but after examining only a few dolls known to have hard plastic characteristics and comparing them with known composition and vinyl dolls, you will be able to distinguish these differences.

Complete bibliographical data on books used for references plus additional source material will be found in the Bibliography at the end of this book.

The authors realize that not every hard plastic doll is listed here. However, one of the joys of research is finding and identifying new additions to one's collection. Happy Hunting!

The abbreviation "HP" for hard plastic has been used throughout this book.

SYSTEM USED FOR PRICING DOLLS

Prices in this book reflect a range of prices from various parts of the United States. These prices are only given for the specific dolls photographed. These dolls would be in *good* to *mint* condition and include original clothes. There would be higher prices for a doll with an original box, tag and/or "tissue" mint conditions. Local prices will vary.

If a doll is scarce or very rare, it will be costly. Where dolls are still "coming out of attics" or "readily available at garage sales," prices will be lower. Personality dolls are usually more expensive.

Because clothes were important to society in the 1950s, these dolls often had elegant and lovely clothes. Even everyday clothes were fancy and surprisingly well made. As with all dolls, unusual clothes will add to the quoted prices. Undressed dolls are usually worth 1/4 to 1/3 the value of a dressed doll.

Hard plastic dolls were still available in quantity three to four years ago. Today the collector sees fewer and fewer in mint condition and prices have risen. It is not at all uncommon to see unheralded, rare dolls go for remarkable prices at auction, especially when in mint condition. The Nancy Ann *Style Show* doll is an example.

Because of the extremely firm, hard quality of the plastic and improved mold techniques, a doll artist could sculpt lovely figures in fine detail, and they could be manufactured in quantity. Some of these wonderful dolls have now become truly objects of art.

A & H

History:

Hard plastic was an exciting invention in the late 1940s and early 1950s. The material allowed the doll artist to sculpt with more detail than with composition, and the dolls could be produced in quantities inexpensively.

A & H used mass advertising in magazines to promote dolls of the new material. One of these magazines was *McCalls Needlework Magazine*. The company was successful because of a tremendous demand for all types of toys. Few dolls and toys were made during the war years.

A & H dolls were fancy, pretty and appealed to adults as well as children. They were relatively inexpensive and made nice gifts. The *Marcie* line was a good seller.

Many of the dolls were unmarked except for their boxes, and most had Plastic Molded Arts characteristics. (See PMA page 207) However, some of them had Virga-Beehler Arts characteristics.

Most of the dolls were meant to be displayed, but some of the *Marcie* line had extra clothes which could be purchased and used for play. These dolls competed with *Ginny*.

Gigi: HP; 7½in (19.1cm); came in other sizes; jointed knee walker with turning head; wigs; jointed neck, arms, legs; sleep eyes; came with extra outfits to purchase; circa 1953.

    MARKS: Unknown; none

    SEE: *Illustration 1*; reprint of *McCalls Needlework Magazine*, Fall/Winter 1955. *(Pat Parton Collection.)*

    PRICE: $15-20

Gigi: Vinyl head; HP; 7½in (19.1cm); rooted hair; jointed neck, arms, legs, knee; walker; came with different outfits and accessories; sleep eyes; closed mouth; sits, stands, walks, sleeps; circa 1955.

    MARKS: Unknown; none

    SEE: *Illustration 2;* reprint from *McCalls Needlework Magazine, Fall/Winter 1955-1956. (Pat Parton Collection.)*

    PRICE: $15-20

Illustration 1.   *Illustration 2.*

Illustration 3.   Illustration 4.

Girl: HP; 8in (20.3cm); typical PMA characteristics, see page 207; PMA shoes with bow (see Identification Guide, page 283A); standard arm hook with unusual ridge (see Identification Guide [Arms], page 264I); closed mouth; fingers molded together at bottom, but separate near top; green net dress with yellow ribbon trim; green felt hat; molded eyelashes; circa 1953.
MARKS: None on body; "A & H Woodside 77, N.Y." on bottom of plastic see-through box
SEE: *Illustration 3.*
PRICE: $5-9

Mexican Girl: HP; 10½in (26.7cm); jointed at neck, arms, legs; molded shoes with bow (see Identification Guide, pages 283A and 287N); closed mouth; second and third fingers on each hand molded together; mold mark through middle of ear; painted prominent eyelashes below the eye; sleep eyes with molded lashes; beige dress with Mexican figures; green felt hat with red fringe; circa 1953.
MARKS: "Pat's Pending" (back)
SEE: *Illustration 4.*
PRICE: $10-15

Marcie Doll: These dolls were both the name of a specific doll and the brand name used of other types of dolls. In the *McCall's Needlework Magazine*, Spring/Summer 1952, they advertised 7½in (19.1cm) hard plastic dolls with movable arms and heads. They had wigs and sleep eyes. Pictured in their advertisement was *Little Gypsy*, *Gibson Girl*, *Flower Girl* and *Floradora*. Circa 1953.
MARKS: Unknown
PRICE: $15-25

Alice and Her Book: a Marcie doll: HP: 7½in (19.1cm). The doll came with *The Wonder Book Alice in Wonderland*. The book and the doll came in the same box. Circa 1953.
MARKS: Unknown
SEE: *Illustration 5*; reprint of a brochure found in a Marcie doll box. *(Marie Ezzo Collection.)*
PRICE: $15-30

802 *Bride*
805 *Senorita*
807 *Pinafore Alice*
810 *Carmen*
835 *Negro Bride*
813 *Venetian Lady*
809 *Flower Girl*
801 *Colonial Girl*
849 *Floradora*
814 *Dutch Girl*
819 *Charmette*
808 *Marigold*
806 *Annabelle*
811 *Spring*
860 *Drum Major*
859 *Girl Graduate*
853 *Fatima*
817 *Sweetheart*
818 *Colleen*
824 *Easter Parade*
829 *Stardust*
826 *Norwegian Lass*
827 *Swedish Maid*
821 *Daisy*
822 Florentine Girl
839 *Nurse*
823 *Glamour Girl*
825 *Gibson Girl*
832 *Majorette*
834 *Calypso*
830 *Ballerina*
854 *Canasta Girl*
855 *Robin Hood*
856 *Maid Marian*
840 *Debutante*
845 *Miss Jr. Prom*
850 *Hadassah*
831 *Czech Beauty*
846 *Bubbles*
847 *China Doll*
842 *Cowboy*

No. AW
"Alice and Her Books"

Imagine reading this wonderful story while holding an exact replica of Alice right in your hands.

This is the first of the Marcie "Read and Play" series. Watch for the next one.

Illustration 5.

843 *Cowgirl*
848 *Harlequin*
844 *Ice Skater*
852 *Mardi Gras*
851 *Roller Skater*

857 *Miss Poland*
858 *Casablanca*
861 *George*
    Washington
862 *Happy Birthday*

***Donna Dolls* by Marcie:** HP; 12in (30.5cm); jointed at neck, arms, legs; many different formal costumes; closed mouth; circa 1953.
    MARKS: Unknown
    SEE: *Illustration 6;* reprint from *McCalls Needlework Magazine,* Spring/Summer 1953. *(Pat Parton Collection.)*
    PRICE: $8-12

Illustration 6.

Illustration 8.

Illustration 7.

Illustration 9.

Dutch Girl: HP; 7in (17.8cm); Virga type, see page 240; painted side glancing eyes; Virga-type shoes (see Identification Guide, page 285H); first, second, third, fourth fingers molded together; blue satin dress, white lace apron and blouse, white lace Dutch hat; circa 1953.

    MARKS: None; label reads, "The Marcie Doll"

    SEE: *Illustration 7. (Marie Ezzo Collection.)*

    PRICE: $5-7

Priest (see Playhouse Dolls): HP; 7in (17.8cm); sleep eyes; male hair painted on head; molded, painted black shoes with bow (see Identification Guide, page 283B); fingers molded together at bottom but separated at top; circa 1953.

    MARKS: None on body; tab on black cassock, "This is a Marcie Doll"

    SEE: *Illustration 8.*

    PRICE: $5-7

Salvation Army Lad* and *Lass: HP; 8in (20.3cm); blue sleep eyes; closed mouth; molded hair on boy; red wig on girl; dressed in a dark blue Salvation Army uniform; blue cap and bonnet; circa 1953.

    MARKS: None; box labeled "Marcie Dolls Created by A & H Doll Mfg. Corp. Woodside, N.Y., Lad 887, Lass 885"

    SEE: *Illustration 9. (Beatrice Campbell Collection.)*

    PRICE: $15-20 each

14

Illustration 10.   Illustration 11.

Illustration 12.

Ken Murray's TV *Glamour Cowboy*: (see Plastic Molded Arts); HP; 7½in (19.1cm); jointed; shoe (see Identification Guide, page 283B); sleep eyes; dressed as a cowboy. This personality doll represented the famous Glamour Cowboy on the very early television show of the 1950s. The lovely "cowboy" graced the television screen but did not talk. She did turn around to show the abbreviated costume seen in the illustration with the words, "I like the Wide Open Spaces." This doll is particularly interesting because it illustrated the fact that many doll companies purchased dolls from other companies and either costumed them, distributed them or both. The cowboy illustrated in the PMA section is a marked doll with Plastic Molded Arts, L.I.S. New York on the body. The A & H doll is not marked. The only difference between the two dolls is that the Marcie doll is wearing a purple vest and the PMA doll is green; both wear white leather pants with a cowboy hat.

> **MARKS:** None; box labeled "A Marcie Doll;" lariat labeled "Ken Murray TV Glamour Cowboy"
> **SEE:** *Illustration 10. (Marie Ezzo Collection.) Illustration 11. (Marie Ezzo Collection.) Illustration 12. (Marie Ezzo Collection.)*
> **PRICE:** $15-20

Dolls of Destiny: A & H was one of the first companies after World War II to feature historical dolls done in hard plastic with an attempt to authenticate hair and clothes. They were head turning walkers, fully-jointed, 12in (30.5cm), and came with a book telling about each character. The characters were *Queen Victoria, Mary Todd Lincoln, Priscilla Alden, Polly Pitcher, Empress Eugenia, Queen Isabella, Empress Josephine, Marie Antoinette, Betsy Ross, Martha Washington, Queen Elizabeth I* and *Elizabeth Woodville Grey.*

Illustration 12a.

Illustration 12b.

Queen Elizabeth I: HP; 12in (30.5cm); head turning walker; jointed at neck, arms and legs; molded shoes with bow (see Identification Guide, page 283A); closed mouth; second and third fingers on each hand molded together; two dimples on each knee; mold mark through middle of ear; painted prominent eyelashes below the eye; sleep eyes with molded lashes; red hair styled like Elizabeth I; gold brocade dress with pearl necklace and pearls in hair; matching gold brocade cape; beautiful underwear with hoop skirt; circa 1950. Clothes are beautifully detailed and sewn for this type of doll.

    MARKS: "Pat's Pending" (back); label sewn in dress
    SEE: *Illustrations 12a and 12b.*
    PRICE: $30

Dainty Dolly: 8½in (26.7cm) is all HP and resembles *Ginny.* Marcie Dolls: also came as a *Musical Sweetheart* which stands on a revolving music box.

A CTIVE
(Beau Art Company)

Illustration 13.

Illustration 14.

Bride: HP; 5½in (14cm); Beau Art Doll; white satin and lace wedding dress with a white lace veil; Virga characteristics (see Identification Guide, page 240); painted on shoes (see Identification Guide, page 285H); red hair, circa 1955.

    MARKS: None on doll; box marked "Beau Art Dolls Active Doll Corporation"

    SEE: *Illustration 13. (Marie Ezzo Collection.)*

    PRICE: $6-10

Clown: HP; 5½in (14cm); Beau Art Dolls; Virga characteristics (see Identification Guide, page 240); painted on shoes; pink skirt with black net ruffle and blouse; multi-colored hat; circa 1954.

    MARKS: None on doll; box marked "Beau Art Dolls Active Doll Co. New York, N.Y."

    SEE: *Illustration 14. (Marie Ezzo Collection.)*

    PRICE: $6-10

Illustration 15.   *Illustration 16.*

Madame Butterfly: HP; 5½ in (14cm); Beau Art Dolls; Virga characteristics (see page 240); painted on shoes (see Identification Guide, page 285H); white nylon dress with black and yellow ribbon; embroidered gold butterfly on hat; circa 1955.

MARKS: None on doll; box marked "Beau Art Dolls Active Doll Co., New York, N.Y."

SEE: *Illustration 15.*

PRICE: $6-10

Nun: HP; 5½ in (14cm); Beau Art Dolls; Virga characteristics (see page 240); painted on shoes (see Identification Guide, page 285H); black habit with white collar and cross; long black veil; circa 1955.

MARKS: None on body; box marked "Beau Art Dolls Active Doll Co. New York, N.Y."

SEE: *Illustration 16. (Marie Ezzo Collection.)*

PRICE: $6-10

DOLLS NOT PHOTOGRAPHED

Other dolls by Active include *Mindy*, a *Ginny* look-alike and a Queen, 10½ in (26.7cm) adult doll.

ADVANCE

Advance walking dolls from about 1950 charmed the children of that era. They did not need batteries, and their key wind mechanism was strong as can be seen by the many surviving dolls in walking condition.

The clothes were beautiful and sometimes designed by famous designers. *Wanda* was sold as a skier or drum majorette. *Winnie* was dressed as a little girl or a bride.

Wanda the Walking Wonder: HP; 17-19in (43.2-48.3cm); glued on wig; sleep eyes; closed mouth; key wind rollers on bottom of unremovable shoes; head turns and arms swing as she walks; extremely heavy doll; individual fingers; blue dress faded to purple with white lace, matching organdy hat; circa 1949.
> **MARKS:** None
> **SEE:** *Illustration 17. (Private Collection.) Illustration 18* (instructions). *(Private Collection.)*
> **PRICE:** $70-75

Winnie the Wonder Doll: vinyl head; HP body; 24in (61cm); walking, talking; key wind for walking; a button on chest for talking mechanism; individual fingers; sleep eyes with lashes; lashes also painted below eyes; nonremovable shoes with rollers for walking; pink taffeta tunic with striped underskirt; white lace trim; ribbon read "Winnie the Unaided Walking and Talking Doll;" circa 1956. *Winnie* also came in a HP head version before 1956. She had a closed mouth.
> **MARKS:** None
> **SEE:** *Illustration 19* (vinyl head).
> **PRICE HP DOLL:** $85-95
> **PRICE VINYL HEAD DOLL:** $60-75

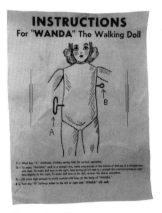

Illustration 18.

Illustration 17.

Illustration 19.

MADAME ALEXANDER

In the late 1940s, Madame Alexander began producing hard plastic dolls. These dolls were manufactured into the 1960s with vinyl and plastic eventually replacing the hard plastic. There were several exceptions. The *Portrette Series*, using the "Cissette" dolls were made into the 1970s, and the small hard plastic "Alexander-kins," are still being manufactured today. The hard plastic Alexander dolls are highly prized by collectors today with their value continually increasing.

Madame Alexander dressed many types of dolls but made very few doll face and body molds. Today, in the identification of Alexander dolls, each face has been given a name such as "Margaret," "Maggie," "Cissy," "Cissette," "Alexander-kins," and so forth. The name for each different face was taken from a popular doll named by Madame Alexander. For example, *Maggie* was the name of a particular hard plastic girl doll who came in a wide variety of outfits. All other dolls that have the same face mold use the term "Maggie" as a means of face identification. When referring to the name of the face mold, it will be in quotes. When referring to the particular name of the doll, it will be italicized.

Along with the totally hard plastic dolls, other types include vinyl headed dolls with hard plastic bodies, hard plastic dolls with vinyl arms, hard plastic bodies with vinyl heads and arms, and babies with hard plastic heads and various other body constructions.

In this section of the book, the dolls are grouped according to the name of the face mold. Before each set of dolls are pictured, there is a short paragraph about the history, markings and the various names of the dolls that use that particular mold.

In considering the price of these Madame Alexander dolls, one should take into account the rarity, the age, the type of costume (the more elaborate the outfit the higher the price) and the condition of the doll and outfit.

Margaret Face Dolls:

The Margaret mold was originally used for the composition dolls of the actress Margaret O'Brien. In 1948, this same face was used to make a mold for hard plastic dolls. It was used through 1956. The earlier dolls were painted hard plastic. The dolls were totally hard plastic with sizes ranging from 14in (35.6cm) to 23in (58.4cm). The arms and legs were straight with flat feet. This series of dolls was very popular, and some of the different characters include; *Babs Ice Skater, Nina Ballerina, Little Women, Godey Fashion Dolls, Queen Elizabeth, Glamour Girl, Alice in Wonderland, Cinderella, Snow White* and *McGuffey Ana*.

MARKS: "Alex" (head); "Alexander" (head); or no markings at all, clothes were usually tagged.

Queen Elizabeth II (Margaret face, close-up): 18in (45.7cm) jeweled tiara; fur-trimmed purple and white cape; jeweled necklace; 1953. (See *Illustration 38* for full view.)

MARKS: None
SEE: *Illustration 20. (Thelma Purvis Collection.)*
PRICE: $500-600 and up

Illustration 20.

Illustration 21.

Illustration 22.

Illustration 24.

Illustration 23.

Illustration 25.

Princess Margaret Rose (Margaret face): HP; 14in (35.6cm); lavender dress; straw hat; missing a ribbon around the waist; circa 1952.

MARKS: None; tagged dress
SEE: *Illustration 21.*
PRICE: $300-400

Snow White (Margaret face): HP; 15in (38.1cm); black wig; gold bodice; gold print dress with stand up collar; pink hair ribbon; 1952.

MARKS: "Alex" (head)
SEE: *Illustration 22. (Marianne Gardner Collection.)*
PRICE: $375-400

Prince Charming (Margaret face): HP; 14in (35.6cm); short, curly auburn wig; off-white brocade outfit with gold trim, white cap and tights; circa 1950.

MARKS: None
SEE: *Illustration 23. (Marianne Gardner Collection.)*
PRICE: $525-575

Bride (Margaret face): HP; 17½in (44.5cm); white satin gown; jeweled bodice; white veil with a crown of flowers; circa 1952.

MARKS: "Alexander"
SEE: *Illustration 24.*
PRICE: $225-275

McGuffey Ana (Margaret face): HP; 14½in (36.9cm); blue corduroy coat with brown fur; blue muff; pink bonnet; early Alexander wrist tag; circa 1948.

MARKS: "Alex" (head); tagged dress; wrist tag (green clover)
SEE: *Illustration 25. (Helen Krielow Collection.)*
PRICE: $325-385

Margaret O'Brien (Margaret face):
HP; 18in (45.7cm); walker; yellow
pinafore; straw hat; brown wig; circa
1948.
MARKS: None
SEE: *Illustration 26. (Private
Collection.)*
PRICE: $500 plus

Groom (Margaret face), also *Prince
Phillip:* HP; 17in (43.2cm); black
formal dress; either brown fur wig or
caracul wig; "diamond" stick pin; circa
1952.
MARKS: "Alexander" (head)
SEE: *Illustration 27. (Marianne
Gardner Collection.)*
PRICE: *$500-600*

Illustration 26.

Illustration 27.

Cynthia (Margaret face): HP; rare
black doll; 15in (38.1cm); original
pink taffeta dress with blue belt;
walker; circa 1952-1953.
MARKS: "Alex" (head)
SEE: *Illustration 28. (Jackie
Kaner Collection.)*
PRICE: $500-600

Illustration 28.

Maggie Face Dolls:
Maggie face dolls were produced from 1949 through 1956 and were totally hard
plastic. They came in various sizes from 14in (35.6cm) to 23in (58.4cm) and were both
walkers and non-walkers. The arms and legs were straight and the doll had flat feet.
Maggie was a popular doll and came as *Maggie, Maggie Walker, Little Women, Polly
Pigtails, Annabelle, Godey Ladies, Babs, Peter Pan* and others.
MARKS: "Alex" (head); "Alexander" (head); or none; clothes usually had an
Alexander label

Maggie (close-up): HP; 18in
(45.7cm); one of Queen Elizabeth's
Court Ladies (see *Illustration 37* for a
full view); dark rose cape; pearl neck-
lace, tiara and earrings; circa 1953.
MARKS: None
SEE: *Illustration 29. (Thelma
Purvis Collection.)*

Maggie (Maggie face): HP; 14in
(35.6cm); purple jumper with a white
blouse; came with a variety of outfits
that could be purchased separately;
circa 1951.
MARKS: None
SEE: *Illustration 30.*
PRICE: $200-300

Illustration 29.

Illustration 30.

Illustration 31. *Illustration 32.* *Illustration 33.*

Illustration 34. *Illustration 35.* *Illustration 36.*

Maggie Fashion Brochure: booklet of outfits that could be purchased for the *Maggie* doll.
    SEE: *Illustration 31. (Private Collection.) Illustration 32. (Private Collection.) Illustration 33.* (Gold Medal Award.) *(Private Collection.)*

Peter Pan (Maggie face): HP; 15in (38.1cm); green tunic; green felt hat; brown felt shoes; red hair; original tag; Walt Disney character; 1953.
    MARKS: Wrist tag
    SEE: *Illustration 34. (Marianne Gardner Collection.)*
    PRICE: $450 plus

Alice in Wonderland (Maggie face): HP; 17in (43.2cm); blue dress (faded to lavender) with white organdy pinafore; blonde wig; 1950.
    MARKS: None
    SEE: *Illustration 35. (Sandy Strater Collection.)*
    PRICE: $325-375

Polly Pigtails (Maggie face): HP; 14in (35.6cm); mohair wig; red and green plaid dress; red shoes; straw hat; 1949.
    MARKS: Tagged outfit
    SEE: *Illustration 36. (Marianne Gardner Collection.)*
    PRICE: $250-300

Dolls from Queen Elizabeth's Coronation: ───────

In 1953 Queen Elizabeth was crowned Queen of England. During the 1950s Madame Alexander made dolls depicting the coronation, members of her court and members of her family. The doll faces used were Margaret, Maggie and Cissy (named later).

Court Grouping: HP; 18in (45.7cm); upper row from left to right: *Princess Margaret Rose, Queen Elizabeth* and *Court Lady.* Lower row from left to right: *Court Lady* and *Lady Churchill*; 1953.
    SEE: *Illustration 37. (Thelma Purvis Collection.)*

Queen Elizabeth (Margaret face): HP; 18in (45.7cm); jeweled tiara, necklace and bracelet; white brocade dress with blue sash; purple velvet cape with white fur lining; circa 1953.
    MARKS: None
    SEE: *Illustration 38. (Thelma Purvis Collection.)*
    PRICE: $600 plus

Illustration 37.

Princess Margaret Rose (Margaret face): HP; 18in (45.7cm); pink taffeta formal gown; "diamond" tiara; "pearl" necklace and earrings; dark rose sash; circa 1953.
    MARKS: None
    SEE: *Illustration 39. (Thelma Purvis Collection.)*
    PRICE: $600 plus

Lady Churchill (Margaret face): HP; walker; 18in (45.7cm); pink formal dress with jewel-trimmed cape; drop pearl tiara; 1953.
    MARKS: None
    SEE: *Illustration 40. (Thelma Purvis Collection.)*
    PRICE: $600 plus

Illustration 38.   *Illustration 39.*

Illustration 40.

Cissy Face Dolls:

The Cissy face mold was used for several years before the body was changed and before receiving its name, Cissy. These early dolls were made from 1953-1954, using a girl's body with flat feet. They were totally hard plastic and included *Binnie* and *Winnie Walker, Sweet Violet* and *Me and My Shadow*.

Cissy, with a new body, was introduced in 1955 and was produced until 1962. The doll was 20 to 21in (50.8 to 53.3cm) with an adult body and high-heeled feet. She was all-hard plastic with jointed vinyl arms. The knees were also jointed. *Cissy* was both a walker and non-walker.

This new *Cissy* was a high fashion doll with many clothes and accessories. She had a blonde, brown or red glued on wig. Besides the *Cissy* character, other dolls using the same face include *Margot Ballerina, Queen Elizabeth, Scarlett* and *Godey Fashion Doll*.

MARKS: "Alexander" (head)

Illustration 41.   Illustration 42.

Illustration 43.   Illustration 44.

Binnie Walker (Cissy face close-up): HP; 18in (45.7cm); yellow jumper with black and white striped blouse; straw hat; rooted skull cap hair on HP head; 1955.
MARKS: "Alexander" (head)
SEE: *Illustration 41. (Louise Schnell Collection.)*
PRICE: $250-275

Winnie Walker (Cissy face): HP; 15in (38.1cm); blue coat with white collar and buttons; dark blue hat; hatbox and gold tag: "Winner of Fashion Academy Gold Medal Award"; circa 1955.
MARKS: "Alexander" (head)
SEE: *Illustration 42* (doll). *(Private Collection.) Illustration 43* (hatbox and gold tag). *(Private Collection.)*
PRICE: $200-250

Winnie Walker (Cissy face): HP; 25in (64.5cm); blue velvet coat with matching bonnet and shoes; lace-trimmed white socks; circa 1953.
MARKS: "Alexander" (head)
SEE: *Illustration 44. (Sandy Strater Collection.)*
PRICE: $275-300

Cissy (close-up): HP head; 20in (50.8cm); purple straw hat and ribbon; circa 1956.

> MARKS: "Alexander" (head)
> SEE: *Illustration 45. (Thelma Purvis Collection.)*
> PRICE: $175-225 plus

Cissy (Cissy face): HP heads/ bodies/legs; vinyl jointed arms; 20 to 21in (50.8 to 53.3cm); shown in very fashionable 1950s ensembles; circa 1957.

> MARKS: "Alexander" (head); "Mme Alexander" (body)
> SEE: *Illustration 46.* Purple straw hat and ribbon; sunglasses. *(Thelma Purvis Collection.) Illustration 47.* White satin coat; blue taffeta dress; blonde wig. *(Sandy Strater Collection.) Illustration 48.* Green print nylon dress with pink sash; pearl necklace; nylon lace hat; dark brown wig. *(Sandy Strater Collection.)*
> PRICE: $175-300 each

Cissy/Cissette: 20in (50.8cm) and 10in (25.4cm) dolls wearing matching pink robes and nightgowns; blonde wigs; many outfits for these teen fashion dolls match; circa 1957.

> MARKS: *Cissy:* "Alexander" (head) *Cisette:* "Mme Alexander" (body)
> SEE: *Illustration 49.*
> PRICE: *Cissy:* $150-225
> *Cissette:* $150-200

Illustration 45.

Illustration 46.

Illustration 47.

Illustration 48.

Illustration 49.

Mary Louise (Cissy face): HP; 18in (45.7cm); very rare doll; larger doll from the "Me and My Shadow" series; green coat with white lamb's wool trim, orange skirt; braided hair; green hat trimmed with white lamb's wool; circa 1954.

MARKS: "Alexander" (head)
SEE: *Illustration 50* (doll). *(Marianne Gardner Collection.) Illustration 51* (close-up). *(Marianne Gardner Collection.) Illustration 52* (back). *(Marianne Gardner Collection.)*
PRICE: $800 plus

Illustration 50.

Illustration 51.

Illustration 52.

Portrait Series:

In 1961 the *Jacqueline* doll was introduced. She was made in the likeness of Jacqueline Kennedy. It had a vinyl head and used the Cissy hard plastic body. The Portrait series began in 1965 and used the vinyl Jacqueline face with different hair styles and the Cissy body. They are still being produced today. These Portrait dolls are very beautiful with exquisite fashions and are highly collectible today.

Cornelia (Jacqueline face; Cissy body): Portrait doll; vinyl head/arms; HP body; 21in (53.3cm); blonde wig; hot pink long cape; pink dress with matching hat trimmed in white; 1972.

MARKS: "Alexander 1961" (head); wrist tag
SEE: *Illustration 53.*
PRICE: $550

Illustration 53.

Cissette Face Dolls:

Cissette was a small (10 to 11in or 25.4 to 27.9cm) doll with an adult body. She was introduced in 1957 and production continued until 1973. *Cissy*, as the teen fashion doll, was produced into the early 1960s. The Portrette Series began in the 1960s and lasted until the early 1970s. She was totally hard plastic with high-heeled feet and jointed at the knees. Her wig came in blonde, brunette and shades of red. Her facial features and hairstyles changed throughout the years. *Cissette*, as a fashion model, came with many outfits and accessories. Other uses of the Cissette face were:

1. 1960 - *Sleeping Beauty* (Walt Disney character); different body that had straight legs and flat feet.
2. 1960 - *Margot*; she has an upswept hairdo and wore more sophisticated clothes.
3. 1969 - *Tinkerbelle*; part of the "Peter Pan Collection."
4. 1971 - *Brigetta, Louisa* and *Liesl*; part of the "Sound of Music Collection."
   MARKS: "Mme Alexander" (back)

Cissette (close-up): 10in (25.4cm) *Southern Belle*; Portrette Series; white nylon dress with green ribbons; white straw hat; 1971.

> **MARKS:** "Mme Alexander" (back); wrist tag
> **SEE:** *Illustration 54.*
> **PRICE:** $425-480

Cissette (Cissette face): HP; 10in (25.4cm); pink robe and matching nightgown; light brown wig; circa 1957.

> **MARKS:** "Mme Alexander" (back); tagged outfit
> **SEE:** *Illustration 55.*
> **PRICE:** $150-175

Illustration 54.

Illustration 55.

Margot (Cissette face): HP; 10in (25.4cm); white satin evening wear ensemble; dark brown wig; circa 1961.

> **MARKS:** "Mme Alexander" (back)
> **SEE:** *Illustration 56. (Nancy Roeder Collection.)*
> **PRICE:** $350-425

Jacqueline (Cissette face): HP; 10in (25.4cm); brown hair; yellow dress and coat with matching hat; circa 1962.

> **MARKS:** "Mme Alexander" (back)
> **SEE:** *Illustration 57. (Jackie Kaner Collection.)*
> **PRICE:** $500 plus

Illustration 56.

Illustration 57.

Illustration 58.

Illustration 60.

Illustration 62.

Illustration 59.

Illustration 61.

Illustration 63.

"Sound of Music" (Cissette face): These three dolls were part of a collection from the movie, "The Sound of Music." They were made from 1971 to 1973.

> **MARKS:** "Mme Alexander" (back)
> **SEE:** *Illustration 58 (Louisa).* 11in (27.8cm); Tyrolean flowered skirt; black vest; white blouse; white stockings. *Illustration 59 (Brigetta).* 11in (27.8cm) red flowered skirt; black vest; white blouse. *Illustration 60 (Liesl).* 11in (27.8cm); orange dress; green striped pinafore; blonde wig; straw hat with flowers. *(Beatrice Campbell Collection.)*
> **PRICE:** *Louisa* - $320; *Brigetta* - $225; *Liesl* - $260; prices vary due to rarity.

Scarlett-"Portrette Series" (Cissette face): HP; 10in (25.4cm); green taffeta dress with black trim; matching green bonnet; cameo necklace; 1970.

> **MARKS:** "Mme Alexander" (back)
> **SEE:** *Illustration 61. (Beatrice Campbell Collection.)*
> **PRICE:** $425-480

Southern Belle-"Portrette Series" (Cissette face): HP; 10in (25.4cm); white organdy dress with green ribbons; white straw hat; gold heart necklace; 1972 to 1973.

> **MARKS:** "Mme Alexander" (back)
> **SEE:** *Illustration 62.*
> **PRICE:** $425-480

Queen-"Portrette Series" (Cissette face): HP; 10in (25.4cm); white formal gown; red sash; jeweled tiara; 1972 to 1973.

> **MARKS:** "Mme Alexander" (back)
> **SEE:** *Illustration 63. (Beatrice Campbell Collection.)*
> **PRICE:** $425-480

Illustration 65.

Illustration 64.

Illustration 66.

Elise Face Dolls:

Elise was introduced in 1957 and by 1966 she had become a totally vinyl doll. The original *Elise* was 16½in (41.9cm), had a hard plastic head, body and legs and had vinyl arms. She was jointed at the elbows, knees and ankles. She came in a variety of fashion outfits but she was very popular as a bride and ballerina. In 1961, a vinyl head replaced the hard plastic head.

MARKS: "Alexander" (head); "Mme Alexander" (back) sometimes

Elise (close-up): HP head; 16½in (41.9cm) *Elise Ballerina*; pink tutu; crown of pink flowers; dark brown wig; circa 1958.
MARKS: "Alexander" (head)
SEE: *Illustration 64.*
PRICE: $250-300

Elise: HP head/body/legs; vinyl arms; 16½in (41.9cm); light green nylon print formal; pink flowered satin sash; matching garden hat; circa 1958.
MARKS: "Alexander" (head)
SEE: *Illustration 65. (Barbara Comienski Collection.)*
PRICE: $250-300

Elise Bride: HP head; 16½in (41.9cm); white nylon and tulle bridal gown with a flower bouquet; 1959.
MARKS: "Alexander" (head)
SEE: *Illustration 66. (Nancy Roeder Collection.)*
PRICE: $250-300

Lissy Face:

Lissy was introduced in 1956 as a pre-teen doll. She is 11in to 12in (27.9cm to 30.5cm) with medium high-heeled feet, jointed elbows and knees, see Identification Guide, page 262B for a picture of arm hook. She is made completely of hard plastic. She wore teen fashion clothes and also came as a bride and ballerina. In 1959, *Kelly* was issued using the Lissy face, but with a different body. *Kelly*'s body had unjointed straight arms and legs with flat feet. In 1962, *Pamela* was issued using the Lissy face but with straight arms and legs. She was usually sold in gift cases with additional outfits. The "Little Women Series" used the *Lissy* doll from 1957 to 1968. The later dolls had vinyl heads with hard plastic bodies.

> **MARKS:** Usually not marked on doll; clothes are tagged; later vinyl dolls marked "Alexander" on head

Comparison of *Kelly* and *Lissy* (both 12in [30.5cm] dolls have Lissy face): *Kelly*, on left, has straight arms and legs; *Lissy*, on right, has jointed arms and legs with high heeled feet.

> **MARKS:** None
> **SEE:** *Illustration 67. (Louise Schnell Collection.)*

Lissy: HP; 11½in (29.2cm); red polka dot dress with solid red sweater and hat; circa 1956.

> **MARKS:** None
> **SEE:** *Illustration 68. (Nancy Roeder Collection.)*
> **PRICE:** $275-325

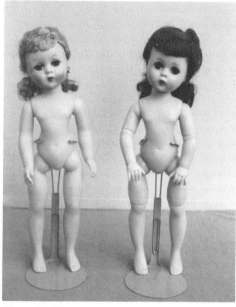

Illustration 67.

Illustration 68.

Lissy Bridesmaid (Lissy face): HP; 11½in (29.2cm); pink nylon dress; circa 1957.
MARKS: None
SEE: *Illustration 69. (Nancy Roeder Collection.)*
PRICE: $275-325

Illustration 69.

"Little Women" (Lissy face): 11½in (29.2cm) dolls; this series included *Meg, Jo, Beth* and *Amy*; they are hard plastic and use the Kelly body; the following "Little Women" are not from the same year; 1958 to 1963.

> **MARKS:** None
> **SEE:** *Illustration 70* (group). *(Louise Schnell Collection.) Illustration 71 (Meg).* Purple and white cotton dress; white organdy apron; purple bow in blonde wig. *(Louise Schnell Collection.) Illustration 72 (Jo).* White cotton dress with black dots; red glazed cotton pinafore. *(Louise Schnell Collection.) Illustration 73 (Beth).* Pink cotton dress; white apron; pink bow in brown wig. *(Louise Schnell Collection.) Illustration 74 (Amy).* White glazed cotton dress; yellow pinafore with white dots. *(Louise Schnell Collection.)*
> **PRICE:** $275-325, except *Laurie* (Lissy face) $375

Marmee: 11in (27.9cm); part of "Little Women" series; green satin dress with white lace shawl collar; yellow apron; 1959. This is a rare doll. Usually the doll is costumed in a dress made of taffeta.

> **MARKS:** "Alexander" (head)
> **SEE:** *Illustration 74a. (Nancy Roeder Collection.)*
> **PRICE:** $275-325

Illustration 70.

Illustration 71.

Illustration 72.

Illustration 73.

Illustration 74.

Illustration 74a.

Wendy, Wendy Ann, Wendy-Kins, and Alexander-Kins:

This small, 7½in to 8in (19.1cm to 20.3cm) all-hard plastic doll was introduced in 1953 and is still being manufactured today. There have been changes in the body construction, flesh color and type of hard plastic used. Also, the names are numerous and often confused and interchanged. These dolls came in a wide variety of costumes and characters. The earliest dolls, from 1953 to 1955, were straight leg walkers and non-walkers. Then the bodies were changed to a bent knee construction that lasted until 1972. From then to the present the dolls have straight legs. Along with little girl clothes there was the "International Series," "Americana Series" and "Storybook Series." In 1955, the Alexander-Kins were used for the "Little Women Series," and they are still being produced today.

MARKS: "Alex" (head); tagged clothes

Quiz-kin (Alexander-Kins):   HP; 8in (20.3cm); straight leg; non-walker; painted hair; not original clothes; push button makes head move "yes" or "no;" 1953.

MARKS: "Alex" (body)
SEE: *Illustration 75. (Nancy Roeder Collection.)*
PRICE: $300-400

Apple Annie (Alexander-Kins):   HP; 8in (20.3cm); straight leg walker; red plaid dress with basket of apples; straw hat; "Americana Series;" 1954.

MARKS: "Alex" (body)
SEE: *Illustration 76. (Aunt Onie Collection.)*
PRICE: Not enough sample prices

Illustration 75.   *Illustration 76.*

Illustration 77.

Billy (Alexander-Kins):   HP; 8in (20.3cm); bent knee walker; blonde wig; beautiful red and white shorts outfit; red hat and tie; circa 1960.

    MARKS: "Alex" (back)

    SEE: *Illustration 77. (Rosemary Romance Collection.)*

    PRICE: $300-350

Illustration 78.

Illustration 79.

Illustration 80.

Wendy Walker (Alexander-Kins): HP; 8in (20.3cm); bent knee walker; blonde wig; blue and white shorts outfit with red tie and belt; blue cap; circa 1958.
MARKS: "Alex" (back)
SEE: *Illustration 78. (Ruth Glover Collection.)*
PRICE: $275-325

Tyrolean Boy (Alexander-Kins): HP; 8in (20.3cm); bent knee; brown hat and shorts; green jacket; red socks; from the "International Series;" circa 1963.
MARKS: "Alex" (back)
SEE: *Illustration 79. (Rosemary Romance Collection.)*
PRICE: $175

Wendy-Kins: HP; 8in (20.3cm); close-up of early straight leg construction; circa 1954.
MARKS: "Alex" (back)
SEE: *Illustration 80. (Barbara Comienski Collection.)*
PRICE: $250 plus

Illustration 81.

Illustration 82.

Nurse (Alexander-Kins):   HP; 8in (20.3cm); bent knee; blue and white striped uniform with a white apron; white hat; came with plastic baby in a white lace gown and hat; 1961.

   MARKS: "Alex" (back)
   SEE: *Illustration 81. (Beatrice Campbell Collection.)*
   PRICE: $700 plus

Marta (Alexander-Kins):   HP; 8in (20.3cm); part of the "Sound of Music Series;" bent knee; white blouse; blue bodice; blue flowered skirt; 1971.

   MARKS: "Alex" (back)
   SEE: *Illustration 82. (Beatrice Campbell Collection.)*
   PRICE: $200

Madelaine:

Madelaine was made during the years 1952 to 1953. She was 18in (45.7cm) tall and Alexander's only ball-jointed doll. She had a vinyl head and a completely jointed hard plastic body with a separate joint at the wrist. She had a blonde wig and is an early example of vinyl. Her open/closed mouth was unique and she came with a beautiful wardrobe; red hair ribbon and dress.

MARKS: "Alexander" (head)
SEE: *Illustration 83* (close-up -- not original). *(Betty Shriner Collection.)*
    Illustration 84. (Wanda Lodwick Collection.)
PRICE: $300-375

Illustration 83.

Illustration 84.

Sleeping Beauty:

Sleeping Beauty was a special doll that was made with the permission of Walt Disney with his name on the wrist tag. There were three sizes made. The first was 10in (25.4cm) tall and used the Cissette body and face. The second was 16½in (41.9cm) tall with a new and different HP head. She used an Elise body. The last size, 21in (53.3cm), used the same HP head as the 16½in (41.8cm) doll, but it used the Cissy body. All had a very yellow wig, blue dress and crown. Most of the blue dresses have faded to shades of pink.

Sleeping Beauty (Cissette): HP; 10in (25.4cm); blue dress has not yet faded; gold lace overbodice and cape; jeweled crown; 1959 to 1960.
    MARKS: "Mme Alexander" (back)
    SEE: *Illustration 85. (Aunt Onie Collection.)*
    PRICE: $375-425

Sleeping Beauty: HP head; 16½in (41.9cm); Elise body; blue faded to purple gown; gold lace cape; diamond jeweled crown; 1959.
    MARKS: "Mme Alexander" (back)
    SEE: *Illustration 86. (Wanda Lodwick Collection.)*
    PRICE: $375 plus

Illustration 85.

Illustration 86.

Shari Lewis Doll:

Alexander's special *Shari Lewis* doll was made in 1959. She had a unique HP head which resembled Miss Lewis. She was made in two sizes. The 21in (53.3cm) size had a HP head and a Cissy hard plastic body with vinyl arms. The 14in (35.6cm) size had the same HP head but with an Elise hard plastic body with vinyl arms. *Shari Lewis* came in several beautifully made outfits.

MARKS: "Alexander"

SEE: *Illustration 87.* 14in (35.6cm); gold brocade dress; pink sash and trim; gold high-heeled shoes. *(Nancy Roeder Collection.)*

PRICE: $360 plus

Illustration 87.

Maggie Mixup:

Maggie Mixup came in two sizes, 8in (20.3cm) and 16in (40.6cm). This cute doll had straight hair, red or blonde, with bangs and freckles. The earlier 16in (40.6cm) had a head made of hard plastic and the later *Maggies* were made of vinyl and plastic. The smaller size used a hard plastic head with a different face on the Alexander-Kins body. The face can have freckles with red or blonde hair.

Maggie Mixup: HP; 8in (20.3cm); dolls often came undressed; the blonde *Maggie* has been dressed by its owner; circa 1960.

MARKS: "Alex" (back)
SEE: *Illustration 88. (Louise Schnell Collection.)*
PRICE: $350-400

Little Genius (baby): HP head; vinyl body; 8in (20.3cm); blonde wig; open nurser mouth; pink and white print outfit; circa 1956-1962.

MARKS: "Alex" (back); tagged outfit, "Little Genius."
SEE: *Illustration 89* (doll/box). *(Rosemary Romance Collection.)*
PRICE: $150-190

Illustration 88.

Illustration 89.

Illustration 90.

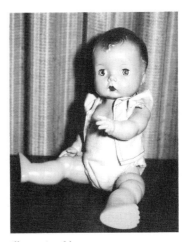

Illustration 91.

Little Genius (baby):   HP head; vinyl body; 8in (20.3cm); blonde wig; open nurser mouth; left doll is wearing white lace diaper with pink and white bonnet; right doll is wearing a pink dress; circa 1956-1962.

    MARKS: "Alex" (back)

    SEE: *Illustration 90. (Ruth Glover and Heloise Miles Collection.)*

    PRICE: $150-190

Precious Toddler/Baby Lovey Dovey: HP; 12in (30.5cm); molded hair; not original clothes; circa 1948.

    MARKS: "Alexander" (head)

    SEE: *Illustration 91. (Rosemary Romance Collection.)*

    PRICE: Not enough samples available.

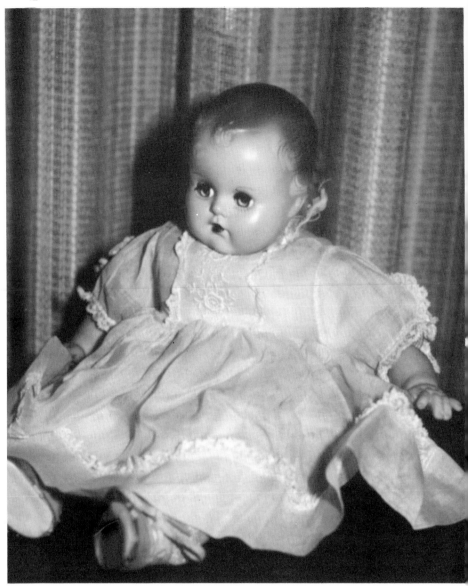

Illustration 92.

Baby: HP head; cloth body; vinyl limbs; 12in (30.5cm); vinyl limbs; original lace-trimmed white dress; molded hair; circa 1951.
    MARKS: "Alexander" (head)
    SEE: *Illustration 92. (Rosemary Romance Collection.)*
    PRICE: $75-125

AMERICAN CHARACTER

Before World War II, this company had made some excellent dolls in composition. An example was the *Petite Sally* doll of the 1920s and 1930s. After the war, they started to make hard plastic dolls, and they were soon turning out some of the loveliest dolls on the market. The company today is no longer in business.

While all American Character dolls are highly collectible, there are three outstanding hard plastic dolls. They are *Betsy McCall, Sweet Sue* and *Tiny Tears*. All three were favorites with children, and they are collector favorites today.

Betsy and *Tiny Tears* are usually well marked but *Sweet Sue* is often totally unmarked. Those that are marked often have the raised letters almost worn off.

American Character is one of the few companies that attempted to use the newly discovered rooted hair on a hard plastic head during the early 1950s. It was accomplished by the use of a skull cap glued onto the head. This process was used for some *Betsy McCall* dolls, some *Tiny Tears* and some *Sweet Sue* dolls. The skull caps were used on the *American Beauty Sweet Sue* teen-type walker with the jointed knees and oversleeve vinyl arms. It was also used on the 24in (61cm) child made of hard plastic.

SEE: *Illustration 93.*

IDENTIFYING MARKS:
1. American Character, Pat. No. 2.675.644.
2. A.C.
3. McCall Corporation (on back in circle).
4. American Character.
5. Amer. Char.

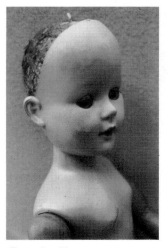

Illustration 93.

Baby Sue: HP head; cloth body; 17in (43.2cm); various other sizes; smooth, pliable latex hands and legs; molded, painted hair or wig; closed mouth; some with cryers; individual fingers; sleep eyes with lashes; not original clothes; 1948 to 1950.

    MARKS: "American Character" (neck); or none

    SEE: *Illustration 94.*

    PRICE: $50-55

Betsy McCall: HP; 8in (20.3cm); beautiful bisque-like finish; rooted brown hair in plastic skull cap covering; or wig; blue sleep eyes with molded lashes; closed mouth; knee joints; second and third fingers molded together; *Betsy* has clothes which could be purchased, and *McCalls Magazine* featured *Betsy* and her wardrobe each month in paper doll form; also many commercial patterns available for this doll; 1958.

    MARKS: "McCall Corporation" (on back in circle)

    SEE: *Illustration 95. Illustration 96* (in box). *(Sandy Strater Collection.) Illustration 97* (sports clothes). *(Louise Schnell Collection.) Illustration 98* (comic book).

    PRICE: $65-95

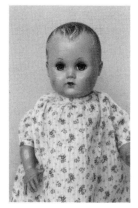

Illustration 94.

Illustration 95.

Illustration 96.

Illustration 97.

Illustration 98. Brochure from the American Doll Corp, New York, New York.

Bride: painted HP; 14in (35.6cm) and other sizes; non-walker; closed mouth; sleep eyes with lashes; mohair wig in early styles; hand slightly curled with third and fourth fingers molded together; lashes painted daintily under eyes; off-white satin dress; veil; petticoat has a hoop; flat feet; shoes and anklet type socks; original clothes; 1950.
>**MARKS:** "A.C." (head)
>**SEE:** *Illustration 99.*
>**PRICE:** $80-95

Illustration 99.

Sweet Sue and *Sweet Suzanne:*_____

These dolls were very popular and there were many variations and sizes throughout the years. The earliest ones in 1949 and 1950 were painted hard plastic but the later dolls had flesh color mixed into the plastic compound. Most of the dolls were unmarked but the face is very easy to identify (see *Illustration 107*). These dolls were made into the late 1950s.

Sweet Sue Characteristics for Easier Identification.
1. Rather light skin color, but there is some blush in the cheeks.
2. The hair is coarse, rough and difficult to curl, but it is pretty and washable.
3. The walkers have a spring in the arm joint which is distinctive to these dolls.
4. Many dresses are full skirted with an attempt to imitate the hoop skirt especially in the formal wear. The sleeves are often puffed below the elbow.
5. Shoes often have a snap closing.
6. Most wigs are blonde or reddish blonde.
7. *Sweet Sue* came as a little girl or as a teen.
8. 2nd and 3rd fingers molded together and 1st finger curled back.

One of the easiest means of identifying a *Sweet Sue* doll is through the clothes, so an unusual number of pictures of the *Sweet Sue* will be shown. These clothes, without the doll, often show up at doll shows, garage sales and flea markets. When added to the proper doll, the value increases.

Bride *(Sweet Sue):* HP; 18in (45.7cm); various other sizes; rooted hair in skull cap glued to head; closed mouth; sleep eyes with lashes; jointed sleeve arms of vinyl and jointed knees; flat feet; original clothes; individual fingers; white satin and lace bridal gown; lace-trimmed veil; circa 1955. There were many *Sweet Sue* brides. They are very beautiful, and they have won many awards at doll competitions. Their clothes have held up well over the years and still look well on the graceful *Sweet Sue.*

    MARKS: "Amer. Char." (head); or none
    SEE: *Illustration 100. (Private Collection.)*
    PRICE: $100-130

American Beauty *(Sweet Sue):* HP; 21in (53.3cm); various sizes; rooted hair in vinyl skull cap glued to head; closed mouth; sleep eyes with lashes; jointed sleeve arms of vinyl and jointed knees; individual fingers; original clothes; pink nylon formal; white flowers around waist; basket of flowers in right hand; flowers in hair; circa 1955.

    MARKS: None
    SEE: *Illustration 101. (Beatrice Campbell Collection.)*
    PRICE: $130-140

Illustration 100.   *Illustration 101.*

Walking Doll *(Sweet Sue):* HP; 14½in (36.9cm); various sizes; closed mouth; sleep eyes with lashes; delicate lashes painted below eyes; individual fingers; arm spring joints; flat feet; original dress came in various colors; wig; head turns as she walks; black print cotton dress; pink collar and sleeves; black cotton coat; circa 1956.
>   **MARKS:** None
>   **SEE:** *Illustration 102* (label). *(Barbara Comienski Collection.) Illustration 103* (label). *(Barbara Comienski Collection.) Illustration 104* (doll/coat).
>   **PRICE:** $75-85

Girl *(Sweet Sue):* see description of walking doll above; original piqué dress that came in several colors; straw bonnet; circa 1953.
>   **MARKS:** None
>   **SEE:** *Illustration 105. (Phyllis Appell Collection.)*
>   **PRICE:** $75-85

Illustration 102.   Illustration 103.

Illustration 104.   Illustration 105.   Illustration 106.

Walking Doll *(Sweet Sue):* HP; 24in (61cm); head turning walker; closed mouth; sleep eyes with lashes; feathered eyebrows; spring in arm joints; skull cap with inserted rooted hair; jointed only at neck, arms, legs; individual fingers; original clothes; peach taffeta dress; black velvet belt with flower; matching hairbows with flowers; circa 1951.
>   **MARKS:** "Amer. Char."
>   **SEE:** *Illustration 106.*
>   **PRICE:** $100-130

Girl *(Sweet Sue):* HP; vinyl arms; 36in (91.4cm); closed mouth; sleep eyes with lashes; fully-jointed wig; not original clothes; circa 1955.
>   **MARKS:** None
>   **SEE:** *Illustration 107. (Rosemary Romance Collection.)*
>   **PRICE:** $120-140

Illustration 107.

Illustration 108.　　　　*Illustration 109.*

Illustration 110.　　　　*Illustration 111.*

Teen *(Sweet Sue)*:   HP; 20in (50.8cm); blue formal with braid in hair; *Sweet Sue* characteristics; skull cap; circa 1951.
　　MARKS: "A.C."
　　SEE: *Illustration 108. (Cindy Bezdek Collection.)*
　　PRICE: $100-120

Teen *(Sweet Sue)*:   HP; 18in (45.7cm); various sizes; walker; wig; *Sweet Sue* characteristics; spring joint arms; hooped underskirt; snap shoes; peach formal with peach lace dropped bodice and ruffled skirt; circa 1953.
　　MARKS: None
　　SEE: *Illustration 109.*
　　PRICE: $100-110

Teen *(Sweet Sue)*:   HP; 18in (45.7cm); walker, *Sweet Sue* characteristics; white dress; hooped underskirt; original clothes; circa 1953.
　　MARKS: "A.C."
　　SEE: *Illustration 110. (Pat Parton Collection.)*
　　PRICE: $100-110

Large Walker *(Sweet Sue)*:   HP; 24in (61cm); *Sweet Sue* characteristics; very popular original dress; circa 1953.
　　MARKS: None
　　SEE: *Illustration 111. (Rosemary Romance Collection.)*
　　PRICE: $110-130

Illustration 112.

Tiny Tears; four variations and sizes; 1950 to 1955.
    SEE: *Illustration 112.*
SEE following illustrations and descriptions.

Tiny Tears: HP head; 18½in (47cm); rubber body which squeeks when pressed; very heavy doll (over four pounds); mouth with hole in it for bottle; sleep eyes with lashes; hole in nostrils close to eyes for tears; dimples above toes on feet and below fingers on hands; original clothes; white playsuit with pink trim; circa 1950.
    MARKS: "American Character" (head)
    SEE: *Illustration 113.*
    PRICE: $70-80

Tiny Tears: HP head; 15in (38.1cm); vinyl body; plastic has waxy look; mouth with hole for bottle; sleep eyes with lashes; holes in nostrils close to eyes for tears; dimples above toes on feet and below fingers on hands; individual fingers; rooted hair inset into skull cap; clothes not original; circa 1952 to 1955.
    MARKS: "American Character, Pat. No. 2.675.644" (head)
    SEE: *Illustration 114.*
    PRICE: $45-50

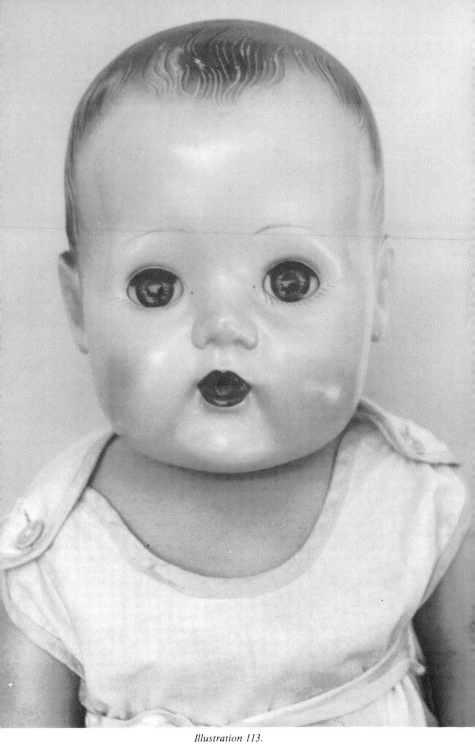

Illustration 113.

Illustration 114.   *Illustration 115.*   *Illustration 116.*

Tiny Tears: HP head; 12in (30.5cm); all rubber body; mouth with hole for bottle; sleep eyes with lashes; holes in nostrils close to eyes for tears; individual fingers with dimples below fingers on hands and dimples above toes on feet; rubber body squeeks when pressed; head measures 11in (27.9cm) in circumference; white and pink cotton dress; circa 1950.

> **MARKS:** "Pat. No. 2.675.644; American Character" (head)
> **SEE:** *Illustration 115.*
> **PRICE:** $45-50

Tiny Tears: HP head; 11in (27.9cm); vinyl arms, legs and body; plastic has waxy look; mouth with hole for bottle; sleep eyes with lashes; hole in nostrils close to eyes for tears; dimples above toes on feet and below fingers on hands; body squeeks when pressed; head 10in (25.4cm) around; individual fingers; aqua dress with white top; circa 1952 to 1955.

> **MARKS:** "Pat. No. 2.675.644 American Character" (head)
> **SEE:** *Illustration 116.*
> **PRICE:** $40-45

DOLLS NOT PHOTOGRAPHED:

American Character made nice baby dolls. *Ricky, Jr.* and the *I Love Lucy Baby* were celebrity dolls of the period. SEE: John Axe, "Modern Doll Mysteries," *Doll Reader,*® November 1982, page 112.

Other babies include an 8in (20.3cm) one-piece doll with the mark "Amer. Char." in a circle on the back. She sometimes came in a lamb rocker.

A special kind of *Sweet Sue* was *Annie Oakley.*

A RRANBEE (R & B)

Before World War II the Arranbee (R & B) Company made composition dolls to compete with Ideal, Alexander, American Character and others. Their composition was excellent and long lasting, and when the company changed to hard plastic in 1947, they continued the excellent quality of their pretty dolls. The wigs used on their dolls were lovely and the hair is easily managed even today. When handled carefully, it usually falls back into the original style.

About 1958 Arranbee was purchased by Vogue Doll Company who continued the R & B line for two years. Vogue sometimes put out the same doll under the two names. An example is the *Littlest Angel* by R & B and the *Li'l Imp* by Vogue. Both dolls are marked on the neck R & B, but come in differently marked boxes.

SEE: *Illustration 117.*
PRICE: $75-90 (rare costumes)
　　　　$35-45 (other)

Nanette and *Nancy Lee:*

These were Arranbee's most common hard plastic dolls. The *Nancy Lee* line was introduced first in the late 1940s, and *Nanette* came soon after. These dolls used their own name, but the same molds were used for other character names in the Arranbee line. *Nanette* continued until 1956. The only way to know the actual name is through a wrist tag. A late *Nanette* doll could also have a vinyl head and HP body.

Most of the dolls were marked "R & B" on the head. "210" was another marking usually combined with the "R & B" mark on the head.

Characteristics of *Nanette* and *Nancy Lee:*

HP; came in various sizes; many beautiful wigs in different colors; closed mouth; various types of hands, but most have 1st, 2nd, 3rd fingers molded together and slightly curled; sleep eyes with lashes; lashes painted under eyes; pointed chin; lovely skin tone with red on cheeks, hands and knees; standard arm joints; delicate sculpture to entire doll; came as boy.

MARKS: "R & B"
SEE: *Illustration 118* (close-up of face).
PRICE: $85-110

Illustration 117.　　　　　　　　　　　　*Illustration 118.*

Illustration 119.

Illustration 120.

Blonde girl: HP; 14in (35.6cm); not original clothes; (see characteristics of *Nanette* and *Nancy Lee*).

    MARKS: "R & B"
    SEE: *Illustration 119. (Pat Parton Collection.)*
    PRICE: $85-110 (in original clothes)

Girl: HP; 14in (35.6cm); original formal fashion clothes; gold brocade dress with fur trim; matching muff; blonde hair (see characteristics of *Nanette* and *Nancy Lee*).

    MARKS: "R & B" (head)
    SEE: *Illustration 120. (Sandy Strater Collection.)*
    PRICE: $90-120

Girl: HP; 14in (35.6cm); wearing red dress with white collar (see *Nanette* and *Nancy Lee* characteristics).

    MARKS: "R & B" (head)
    SEE: *Illustration 121. (Thelma Purvis Collection.)*
    PRICE: $85-110

Illustration 121.

Illustration 122.

Illustration 123.

Girl: HP; 14in (35.6cm); blonde with pigtails; not original clothes (see characteristics of *Nanette* and *Nancy Lee*).

> **MARKS:** "R & B" (head)
> **SEE:** *Illustration 122. (Pat Parton Collection.)*
> **PRICE:** $85-110 (in original clothes)

Girl: HP; 14in (35.6cm) (see *Nanette* and *Nancy Lee* characteristics); red print dress; red pinafore apron with lace; red straw hat; additional clothes included pink flowered gown; red striped shirt and jeans.

> **MARKS:** "R & B" (head)
> **SEE:** *Illustration 123. (Gail Anderson Collection.)*
> **PRICE:** $85-110

Girl: HP; 18in (45.7cm); red dress with white lace; same characteristics as *Nanette* and *Nancy Lee*.

> **MARKS:** "R & B" (head)
> **SEE:** *Illustration 124. (Louise Schnell Collection.)*
> **PRICE:** $85-110

Illustration 124.

Illustration 125.

Illustration 126.

Illustration 127.

Girl: HP; 18in (45.7cm) (see *Nanette* and *Nancy Lee* characteristics); green jumper; blonde hair.
> **MARKS:** "R & B" (head)
> **SEE:** *Illustration 125. (Louise Schnell Collection.)*
> **PRICE:** $85-110

Cinderella (type): HP; 14in (35.6cm) (see *Nanette* and *Nancy Lee* characteristics); blonde hair; white satin dress with overskirt of white net; trimmed in gold.
> **MARKS:** "R & B" (head)
> **SEE:** *Illustration 126. (Rosemary Romance Collection.)*
> **PRICE:** $85-110

Cowgirl: HP; 18in (45.7cm) (see characteristics of *Nanette* and *Nancy Lee*); brown leather outfit; brown stockings, black boots; gun.
> **MARKS:** "R & B" (head)
> **SEE:** *Illustration 127. (Laura Brown Collection.)*
> **PRICE:** $85-110

Identification Notes:

It is wise to check the back of the neck and body of an unmarked doll if it has the characteristics of a R & B doll. Sometimes it is even necessary to take a light pencil rubbing. Often only the & or the top of the R or B can be seen. Sometimes faint lines can be picked up with a magnifying glass. Occasionally, all marks have worn off.

Marks known to be used by Arranbee are R & B, 250, 210, Pat. 2, 537, 598, Pat. Pending on head and right side of underarm; R & B in circle, R & B/49 and R & B 65.

Illustration 128.

Illustration 129.

Illustration 130.

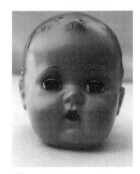

Illustration 131.

Littlest Angel: HP; vinyl head; 10½ in (26.7cm); jointed knee walker; head does not turn; pin jointed (leg joints with pin hidden under body); molded eyelashes; sleep eyes with tiny eyelashes painted under the eyes; dimples on back of hands; rooted hair; open/closed mouth with molded tongue; 2nd and 3rd fingers molded together; circa 1956 to 1959.

> **MARKS:** "R & B/65" (Often this is high on head under rooted hair. In time the mark wears off.); tag reads "Littlest Angel kneels, walks, sits, stands, turns her head. My washable hair is rooted just like real growing hair."
>
> **SEE:** *Illustration 128.* White angel dress with wings trimmed in gold rickrack; gold rickrack halo. *Illustration 129.* White dress; plaid apron with heart-shaped pocket; plaid hat. *(Beatrice Campbell Collection.)*
>
> **PRICE:** $75-90 for *Illustration 128*
> $35-45 for *Illustration 129*

Toddler: HP head; cloth body; vinyl arms and legs; wig; open/closed mouth; sleep eyes with lashes under eyes; dimples on hands; white cotton dress.

> **MARKS:** "250" (head)
>
> **SEE:** *Illustration 130. (Phyllis Appell Collection.)*
>
> **PRICE:** $35-45

Baby: HP head; soft vinyl limbs; stuffed cloth body; molded and painted hair; sleep eyes with lashes; pretty flesh tone with blush on cheeks.

> **MARKS:** "R & B" (head)
>
> **SEE:** *Illustration 131* (doll head). *(Ruth Glover Collection.)*
>
> **PRICE:** $25-30

ARTISAN

The early 1950s were the golden years for hard plastic dolls. Companies were producing high quality dolls of great artistic merit. They were also promoting their beautiful creations by advertising on television which was the wonder of the age.

By 1951 Artisan's 20in (50.8cm) *Raving Beauty*, a non-walker, and *Miss Gadabout*, a different type of walking doll, were featured on television shows in many cities. They modeled the wonderful new post-war fashions, including bathing suits which were now made by well-known designers. Little girls could purchase these suits in miniature for their Artisan dolls.

Other separates included skating costumes, bride's dresses, square dance and cowgirl costumes, day dresses and formals. They also produced underwear and other accessories of the period.

The company, from California, was soon manufacturing these dolls in quantity. However, the advent of vinyl and the beginning of the high-heeled doll soon outmoded these beautiful, long-lasting dolls, by the middle of the 1950s.

These are large dolls. Not only are they 20in (50.8cm) tall, but they were sculpted in larger proportions than other dolls of the period. They foreshadowed the looks of girls today who are often larger than their mothers.

The quality of the hard plastic is excellent and their faces reflect the use of rouge, lipstick and eyeshadow which most women of the time wore. The eyebrows are slightly feathered.

Miss Gadabout featured a walking mechanism which was heavy but allowed the doll to stand and walk and sit with lifelike naturalness. The legs of both dolls are more widely spread than normal and are an easy identification feature (see *Illustration 135*). The dolls are unmarked and are scarce today.

Illustration 132.   *Illustration 133.*

Illustration 134.

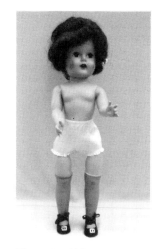

Illustration 135.

Little Miss Gadabout: HP; 20in (50.8cm); felt tongue with four teeth; walker with heavy mechanism; wig that could be washed and curled; sleep eyes with real eyelashes; 2nd and 3rd fingers slightly curled; sit, stand, walk with unusual hip action; red, green and blue rayon taffeta skirt and bolero; white top; 1950 to 1956; $^{o}_{\curlyvee}{}^{o}$ on seat, circa 1950.

> **MARKS:** None on most dolls but this has "Original, Pat. Pending, Heady Turny"
> **SEE:** *Illustration 132. (Laura Brown Collection.) Illustration 133* (markings). *(Laura Brown Collection.)*
> **PRICE:** $80-110

Illustration 136.

Raving Beauty: HP; 20in (50.8cm); fully jointed; Ravon, Dynel hair that can be washed and curled; girl-like breasts; open mouth with felt tongue; four teeth; sleep eyes with real eyelashes; the eyebrows are slightly feathered; individually molded fingers with the 2nd and 3rd slightly curved; $^{o}_{\curlyvee}{}^{o}$ on her seat; two dimples on her elbows; painted knees; flat feet; circa 1950 to 1956. The clothes are original and feature a hoop underskirt, a green satin skirt which was fashionable for formal events and weddings; green striped bodice; nylons with a seam up the back.

> **MARKS:** None
> **SEE:** *Illustration 134* (doll). *(Mavis Mohr Collection.) Illustration 135* (undressed doll). *(Mavis Mohr Collection.) Illustration 136* (face). *(Mavis Mohr Collection.)*
> **PRICE:** $75-100 plus

ASTER

DOLLS NOT PHOTOGRAPHED
The Aster Company made a 20in (50.8cm) all-HP walker that was a *Saucy Walker* look-alike. The doll is unmarked but identified on the box.

BAL DOLLS

Boy: HP; 9in (22.9cm) closed mouth; walking doll with pull string; walks downhill on incline; self-walking when weight is slipped over table; painted side-glancing eyes; molded reddish hair; gauntlet hands; black velvet sailor suit; red tie; matching black tam.
    MARKS: "Made in U.S.A." (lower back); box marked: "General by Bal Dolls, Inc."
    SEE: *Illustration 137.*
    PRICE: $10-15

Illustration 137.

BALLERINAS

During the late 1940s and into the 1950s, there were a great number of dolls dressed as ballerinas, brides, nurses and fashion models. These seemed to be the most common career opportunities then open to girls. However, the most beautiful and magical were the ballerinas. It was during this decade that some of the most beautiful ballerina dolls were produced. They are highly prized and collectible on today's market.

Madame Alexander created possibly the finest ballerina dolls beginning with *Nina Ballerina* in 1949. Many of her later hard plastic dolls came in ballerina outfits.

Illustration 138.

Illustration 139.

Nina Ballerina: HP; 14in (35.6cm); Margaret face; light brown glued on wig; white satin bodice and net overskirt; silver trim; flowers in hair; 1949.
    MARKS: None; dress tagged "Nina Ballerina"
    SEE: *Illustration 138.*
    PRICE: $225-275

Margot Ballerina: HP; by Madame Alexander; 20in (50.8cm); Maggie face; light brown glued on wig; pink bodice with sweetheart neckline; blue organdy skirt; adorned with flowers; circa 1949.
    MARKS: None; tagged dress; early green four-leaf clover wrist tag
    SEE: *Illustration 139.*
    PRICE: $350-400

Illustration 140.

Cissette Ballerina: HP; by Madame Alexander; 10in (25.4cm); glued on light brown wig; Cissette face; beautifully sewn pink satin and tulle tutu; stockings and crown of flowers are missing; jointed at the knees; high heeled feet; circa 1957.

MARKS: "Mme Alexander" (back); tagged Alexander outfit
SEE: *Illustration 140.*
PRICE: $325

Illustration 141.

Illustration 142.

Elise Ballerina: HP head, body, legs; jointed vinyl arms; by Madame Alexander; 16½in (41.9cm); jointed at ankles; pink satin and tulle dress; rhinestone diamond earrings; crown of flowers; Elise face; circa 1958.

    MARKS: "Alexander" (head); "Mme Alexander" (back); tagged dress
    SEE: *Illustration 141.*
    PRICE: $200-250

Elise Ballerina: HP head, body, legs; jointed vinyl arms; by Madame Alexander; 16in (40.6cm); jointed at ankles; metallic gold bodice with a gold tulle skirt; gold slippers; diamond earrings; gold rickrack headdress; Elise face; 1959.

    MARKS: "Alexander" (head); "Mme Alexander" (back); tagged outfit
    SEE: *Illustration 142. (Private Collection.)*
    PRICE: $225-250

Illustration 143.

Illustration 144.

Elise Ballerina: HP head, body, legs; jointed vinyl arms; by Madame Alexander; 16½in (41.9cm); jointed at ankles to enable her to dance on her toes; pink satin and tulle dress; Elise face; circa 1958.

    MARKS: "Alexander" (head); "Mme Alexander" (back); wrist tag

    SEE: *Illustration 143. (Louise Schnell Collection.) Illustration 144.* (wrist tag). *(Louise Schnell Collection.)*

    PRICE: $200-250

Illustration 145.

Ballerina: HP; by Madame Alexander; 10in (25.4cm); rare; outfit and hairdo are for *Cissette* No. 735 from 1963, but this doll came from the factory with Jacqueline or Margot face due to the eye shadow. Purchased in 1965 with "Cissette" marked on box. Ballerina No. 735 should not have the eye shadow.

   MARKS: "Mme Alexander" (back); wrist tag

   SEE: *Illustration 145. (Nancy Roeder Collection. Photograph by Margaret Mandel.*

   PRICE: $350

Illustration 146.

Sweet Sue Ballerina: HP; by American Character; 14½in (36.9cm); pink metallic bodice with a pink tulle tutu; straight legs with flat feet; coarse light brown wig; 2nd and 3rd fingers molded together; child body; circa 1954.
MARKS: None
SEE: *Illustration 146.*
PRICE: $70-85

Illustration 147.

Illustration 148.

Ballerina: HP; by Arranbee; 14in (35.6cm); blue satin and tulle dress; blonde wig with braided hair style; crown of flowers; deep flesh coloring; painted hard plastic; 1st, 2nd, 3rd fingers molded together; circa 1952.
 MARKS: "R & B" (head)
 SEE: *Illustration 147.*
 PRICE: $80-100
Ballerina: HP; by Arranbee; 14in (35.6cm); pink dress with silver trim; elaborate blonde wig; pink net and flowered headdress; painted hard plastic; circa 1953.
 MARKS: "R & B" (head)
 SEE: *Illustration 148. (Barbara Comienski Collection.)*
 PRICE: $80-100

Illustration 149.

Illustration 150.

Illustration 151.

Illustration 152.

Illustration 153.

Ballerina Belle: vinyl head/arms; HP body/legs; by Belle; 21in (53.3cm); walker; rooted light brown hair; jointed knees and ankles; pink tutu and stockings; pink crown of flowers; sleep eyes; circa 1956.

> **MARKS:** "AE/200/21"
> **SEE:** *Illustration 149. (Mary Jane Poley Collection.)*
> **PRICE:** $30-45

Ginger Ballerina: HP; by Cosmopolitan; 7½in (19.1cm); walker; glued on blonde wig; yellow tutu; matching yellow shoes; circa 1957.

> **MARKS:** None; tagged dress "Fashions for Ginger//Cosmopolitan Doll & Toy//Jamaica N.Y.//Trademark."
> **SEE:** *Illustration 150.*
> **PRICE:** $30-45

Ballerina: vinyl head; HP body; by Eegee; 19in (48.3cm); jointed at knees and ankles; large sleep eyes; white tutu with gold trim; circa 1957.

> **MARKS:** "Eegee" (head)
> **SEE:** *Illustration 151. (Pat Parton Collection.)*
> **PRICE:** $30-45

Honey Ballerina: vinyl head; HP body; by Effanbee; straight legs; 19in (48.3cm); saran rooted brown hair; sleep eyes; individually molded fingers; original pink satin and white tulle tutu trimmed with pink and green flowers; circa 1957.

> **MARKS:** "Effanbee" (head)
> **SEE:** *Illustration 152.*
> **PRICE:** $95-110

Honey Ballerina: HP; by Effanbee; 18in (45.7cm); knees and ankles jointed; white tutu with pink flower; circa 1953.

> **MARKS:** "Effanbee" (head)
> **SEE:** *Illustration 153. (Barbara Comienski Collection.)*
> **PRICE:** $125-150

Junior Miss: vinyl head/ arms; HP body; by Effanbee; 18in (45.7cm); white tutu and stockings; pink slippers; circa 1958. An advertisement for the company said, "Plastic body and legs, vinyl arms and head, jointed legs, sleep eyes, Saran hair that can be washed and set; wears net ballerina costume with nylon stockings and ballerina slippers; has decorations in her hair, carries acetate hatbox containing leotard and walking shoes."

This doll is a transitional doll of the late 1950s with a distinctive hard plastic which had not yet crossed over to rigid vinyl. Most of the other new Effanbee dolls of that year were Rigidsol vinyl or all vinyl. For Effanbee, this was the end of a beautiful decade of hard plastic dolls.

MARKS: "Effanbee" (head)
SEE: *Illustration 154.*
PRICE: $95-110

Illustration 154.

Illustration 155.

Illustration 156.

Junior Miss: vinyl head/arms; HP body; by Effanbee; 18in (45.7cm); white dress with a red practice leotard; circa 1958.

MARKS: "Effanbee" (head)

SEE: *Illustration 155. (Barbara Comienski Collection.)*

PRICE: $95-110

Ballerina: vinyl head; HP body/legs; plastic arms; by Horsman; 16½in (41.9cm); jointed at ankles; white tutu; circa 1956.

MARKS: "Horsman"

SEE: *Illustration 156. (Barbara Comienski Collection.)*

PRICE: $40-50

Mary Hoyer Ballerina:.HP; by Mary Hoyer; 14in (35.6cm); light brown glued on wig; closed mouth; 2nd and 3rd fingers molded and curled; white porcelain-like skin color; sleep eyes with lashes; turquoise satin and net dress made from original pattern trimmed with sequins; circa 1948.

> **MARKS:** "Original Mary Hoyer Doll" (in circle on back)
> **SEE:** *Illustration 157.*
> **PRICE:** $125-225 (local prices vary greatly)

Toni Ballerina: HP; by Ideal; 14in (35.6cm); closed mouth; sleep eyes; individually molded fingers; dark, pretty flesh tone; washable hair that could be styled; pink tutu made from an original commercial pattern; circa 1953.

> **MARKS:** "Ideal Doll P-90"
> **SEE:** *Illustration 158.*
> **PRICE:** $55-70

Little Sister Goes to Dancing School:
HP; by Nancy Ann; 4½in (11.5cm); left: black satin dress with black net overskirt and hot pink ribbon trim; right: white outfit with net overskirt; circa 1951.

> **MARKS:** "Nancy Ann Story Book Dolls, U.S.A. Trademark Reg."
> **SEE:** *Illustration 159. (Marianne Gardner Collection.)*
> **PRICE:** $20-35

Illustration 158.

Illustration 157.

Illustration 159.

Illustration 160.

Illustration 161.

Ballerina: HP; by Plastic Molded Arts; 12in (30.5cm); red and white brocade with blue skirt and gold trim; hat is of same brocade; PMA characteristics; circa 1954.
MARKS: None
SEE: *Illustration 160. (Pat Parton Collection.)*
PRICE: $20-30

Terri Lee Ballerina: HP; by Terri Lee; 16in (40.6cm); glued on blonde wig; long blue dress with blue tulle overskirt; gold slippers; circa 1953.
MARKS: "Terri Lee Pat. Pending"
SEE: *Illustration 161.*
PRICE: $150-175

Illustration 162.

Illustration 163.

Ballerina: HP; unknown manufacturer; 8in (20.3cm); jointed at knees with high-heeled feet; walker; glued on red wig; pink and silver metallic tutu; sleep eyes; painted eyelashes; 2nd and 3rd fingers molded; circa 1956.

    MARKS: None

    SEE: *Illustration 162.*

    PRICE: $10-15

Ballerina: vinyl head; HP body/legs; by Valentine; 21in (53.3cm); jointed knees and ankles; gold metallic bodice with a purple skirt; individually molded fingers; muscular upper legs; original stand; closed mouth; sleep eyes; heavily rouged cheeks; walker; navel with dot in center; circa 1958.

    MARKS: "VW 18" (head)

    SEE: *Illustration 163.*

    PRICE: $30-45

Illustration 164.

PAGE 72

Ballerina: vinyl head/arms; curved in a dance pose; HP body; by Valentine; walker with ridge, (see Identification Guide, page 291D); slight depression for navel; closed mouth; individually molded fingers; jointed at knees and legs; flat face; pretty hair pulled back; original silver bodice; blue net skirt with black and gold trim; vinyl slippers with "Capezio" on the bottom; circa 1958.
MARKS: "B 16VW"
SEE: *Illustration 164.*
PRICE: $30-45

PAGE 74

Ballerina: vinyl head/arms; HP body/legs; by Valentine; 18in (45.7cm); closed mouth; sleep eyes with lashes; individually molded fingers with painted nails; jointed at knees and ankles; flat face; walker with ridge, (see Identification Guide, page 291D); original red tutu with vinyl slippers marked "Capezio;" white feather band in hair; circa 1958.
MARKS: None
SEE: *Illustration 165.*
PRICE: $30-45

Illustration 166.

Ballerina: vinyl head; HP body; by Valentine; 14in (35.6cm); distinctive jointed ankles; 2nd and 3rd fingers molded together; walker with ridge, (see Identification Guide); closed mouth; clothes not original; circa 1958.
MARKS: "Made in U.S.A. Pat. Pending" (back)
SEE: *Illustration 166.*
PRICE: $30-45

Ginny **Ballerina:** HP; by Vogue; 7½in (19.1cm); bending knee walker; blonde wig; pink and white tutu; circa 1957.
MARKS: "Vogue" (head); "Ginny//Vogue Dolls Inc.//Pat. No. 2687594//Made in U.S.A."
SEE: *Illustration 167.*
PRICE: $85-110

Illustration 167.

Illustration 165.

DOLLS NOT PHOTO[...]

Many different c[...]
turers made the pop[...]
dolls. The bodies we[...]
were probably made i[...]
tory according to Ruth[...]
doll authority. To det[...]
which company made [...]
doll, it is often neces[...]
marked box. Other [...]
Perfect Companion [...]
Walker.

BEAU ART DOLLS

(See Active Company)

BED DOLLS

In the 1920s and the 1930s, the bed doll was a popular art object for the interior decorator. The unusual shape and style of the elongated bed doll was droll and amusing to that generation. Most of the dolls were composition, although Lenci and others created beautiful cloth and felt dolls.

After World War II, some hard plastic bed dolls were made. They were still decorative but the craze had run its course. However, probably these later dolls will survive as examples of the type because the composition deteriorates and crazes. These dolls are usually unmarked.

Bride: HP head, arms, feet; cloth body; closed mouth; applied eyes on painted white of eye; individual fingers; extremely arched eyebrow; white satin gown with ruffled skirt and hat.
    MARKS: None
    SEE: *Illustration 168. (Lillian Sakal Collection.)*
    PRICE: $45-60

Lady: HP head/arms; cloth body; closed mouth; heavy eyebrows, lashes, and eye shadow; brown eyes; mohair wig; mature figure; pink satin dress and hat; lace trim; good example of later bed dolls.
    MARKS: None
    SEE: *Illustration 169. (Private Collection.)*
    PRICE: $45-60

BRIAN[...]

Brian Swim Doll: [...]
Brian propels hims[...]
    MARKS: "Br[...]
    SEE: *Illustrat[...]*
        Appell Coll[...]
    PRICE: $20-[...]

Illustration 168.

Illustration 169.

BEEHLI

Beehler Arts L
cross references).

Howdy Doody:
hair; red polka dot
   MARKS: Nor
   SEE: *Illustrat.*
     Collection.)
   PRICE: $30-4

DOLLS NOT PH

Another doll b
knees. *Chi Chi* i
Schiaparelli.

Illustration

BELL

Twixie, the T
elbows, knees.
rooted hair; in
shoes or ballet
veil; pearl eart
   MARKS:
   SEE: *Illu*
   PRICE:

CORRINE CREATIVE ARTS

Bride dolls were very popular during the 1950s. Often individuals or companies purchased doll bodies in bulk from doll manufacturing companies, made the costumes and sold them.

A brochure in the boxed doll pictured Mrs. Corrine Friedman of the Bronx, New York, and told about her unique hobby of making doll brides of all nations. "These dolls were dressed authentically in the typical wedding costumes of more than 50 different nations. The originals are valued at several thousand dollars and have been shown in libraries, hospitals, orphanages, and department stores in many parts of the country."

Thirty-one different countries were available including America, Austria, Brazil, Burma, China, Czech, Denmark, Egypt, England, Finland, France, Germany, Greece, Holland, Hungary, India, Ireland, Israel, Italy, Japan, Korea, Mexico, Norway, Panama, Poland, Scotland, Siam, Spain, Sweden, Switzerland and the U.S.S.R. Each doll had a wrist tag which said, "Brides of all Nations, costumed and styled by Corrine."

Girl: 7in (17.8cm) *U.S.S.R Bride;* sleep eyes with molded lashes; PMA characteristics and shoes (see Identification Guide, page 283A); fingers molded together at bottom but separated at top; red hat, vest and skirt; gold apron, white lace blouse; multi-colored trim.
   MARKS: None on body; tag "Brides of all Nations/a hand finished authentically costumed/styled by Corrine."
   SEE: *Illustration 179.*
   PRICE: $8-15

Girl: HP; 7in (17.8cm); same characteristics as *U.S.S.R. Bride* doll; white outfit; lace hat with red and blue flowers; silver trim; multi-colored braid.
   MARKS: None on body; no tag on doll
   SEE: *Illustration 180.*
   PRICE: $8-10

Illustration 179.

Illustration 180.

COSMOPOLITAN

Although Cosmopolitan made many dolls, they are best known for their *Ginger* dolls which are very popular with today's collectors. *Ginger* competed with the Vogue *Ginny*, and she had many, many clothes and accessories which could be purchased separately.

HINTS ON IDENTIFICATION OF *GINGER:* The molded arm hook where it is strung to the body is a very distinctive feature of *Ginger* (see Identification Guide, page 266N). However, it must always be remembered that the elastic in these dolls does wear out and arms were lost and replaced by similar arms that may not be original. *Ginger* has a dimple on her chin, dimples for knuckles on the hand and dimples above her toes.

The authors hope that the information about arms, legs and bodies in this book can be used not only for authenticity, but also will help in repair.

Ginger: HP; 8½in (21.6cm); this size is rarer than the more common 7½in (19.1cm); mold seam through the middle of the ear making the center part of the ear higher than the top and lobe; closed mouth; navel very faint; large round eyes, but the early ones had smaller eyes; dimple under lip that is distinctive; toes all the same length; dots above toes; some have jointed knees with crease in front ankle; all fingers separate; mold flaw at wrist on palm side; fingernails and joint details are excellent; head turning walker; glued on wig; distinctive arm hook (see Identification Guide, page 266N); right: brunette hair; long pink dress with white net overskirt trimmed in blue. Left: blonde hair; purple nylon dress with white lace. Circa 1955.

MARKS: None
SEE: *Illustration 181. (Pat Parton Collection.)*
PRICE: $35-45

Ginger: HP; 7½in (19.1cm); purple hair; various unusual shades of hair color were found on *Ginger;* see characteristics of 8½in (21.6cm) *Ginger;* white dress and hat with colored print; circa 1956.

MARKS: None
SEE: *Illustration 182. (Pat Parton Collection.)*
PRICE: $35-40

Illustration 181.

Illustration 182.

***Ginger* Gift Box:** HP; 7½in (19.1cm); *Ginger* came boxed as a present for a little girl. She came with a variety of outfits, shoes, glasses, roller skates and other accessories.

MARKS: None

SEE: *Illustration 184* (gift box). *(Barbara Comienski Collection.) Illustration 183* (end of box). *(Barbara Comienski Collection.)*

PRICE: $50-75

Gingers: Totally hard plastic doll, 7½in (19.1cm), is on the left; a vinyl head, hard plastic body *Ginger* is on the right; doll on left: white dress with colored polka dots and straw hat; doll on right: purple dress with white lace trim and straw hat; same characteristics as the 8½in (21.6cm) *Ginger*, circa 1956.

MARKS: None on HP doll; "Ginger" (head) of vinyl doll; clothes are tagged "Fashions for Ginger// Cosmopolitan Doll & Toy Co// Jackson Heights N.Y."

SEE: *Illustration 185.*

PRICE: $35-40 and up to $75 for HP *Ginger* in more elaborate or rare outfits. $25-35 for vinyl head *Ginger*; up to $55 for more elaborate outfits.

Ginger (dressed by Terri Lee): HP; 7½in (19.1cm); walker; blue sleep eyes; 1956 to 1958. See characteristics of 8½in (21.6cm) *Gingers*; dressed in Girl Scout or Brownie outfit made by Terri Lee.

MARKS: None; tagged "Terri Lee" on the dress; box labeled "Terri Lee Sales Corporation"

SEE: *Illustration 186. (Ginger* with Terri Lee doll.)

PRICE: $45-55

DOLLS NOT PHOTOGRAPHED

Other dolls by this company include *Baby Emily, Pam Baby, Jeanette,* and *Gloria.* They also made a kit, *Make-Ur-Own Walking Doll Kit,* a 10in (25.4cm) fashion doll.

Illustration 183.

Illustration 184.

Illustration 185.

Illustration 186.

DESOTA DOLLS

Desota made HP, 14in (35.6cm) girl dolls marked "Made in USA" on the back with an accompanying tag marked "Desota Dolls." They also made a *Heart Beat Baby* with a HP head, cloth body and latex limbs. When you lay her down, you can hear her heart beat. Outfit is tagged.

DOLL BODIES

Doll Bodies, Inc. made inexpensive dolls for the mass market. An excellent seller was an 18in (45.7cm) walking doll with dark eyelashes under her eyes. She had dynel hair that was washable, brushable, combable and curlable and came with an assortment of 18 different dresses.

Mary Lu was a 7in (17.8cm) walking doll of the *Ginny*-type. She had the same characteristics as the Roberta doll, (see Identification Guide, pages 264H and 286K). Twenty different dresses with matching panties were sold separately. The doll sold for 89 cents and the dresses were 39 cents. Little girls loved the boxed make-up kit with travel trunk and two extra dresses.

Lingerie Lou was marketed in many ways, but the doll in a home sewing kit was one of their best sellers. During this era, crocheted clothes were very popular, and today the doll is often found wearing the clothes so lovingly created.

Sometimes the company competed with such companies as Ideal who made a small *Mary Hartline* doll. *Lingerie Lou* and *Mary Hartline* wear almost identical costumes, but a comparison shows differences.

Several pattern companies made patterns for this popular doll, and Doll Bodies marketed a special pattern which gave directions for 16 costumes for dolls of all nations (see page 205).

Lingerie Lou (undressed for home sewing): HP; 7½in (19.1cm); sleep eyes; no lashes on eyes; painted eyelashes above eyes; jointed at neck, arms, legs; came with two costume patterns and sewing instructions; 2nd and 3rd fingers molded together; arm hook (see Identification Guide, page 284D); painted shoes (see Identification Guide, page 284D).

MARKS: "Lingerie Lou" (back)
SEE: *Illustration 187. (Pat Parton Collection.)*
PRICE: $5-10

Illustration 187.

Girl-*Lingerie Lou:* HP; 7in (17.8cm); sleep eyes with no lashes; painted lashes above eyes; PMA characteristics; 2nd and 3rd fingers molded together; beautiful detail on hands; dimples below fingers; hand crocheted green doll dress with white angora trim; one-piece body; jointed at neck and arms only; arm hook, (see Identification Guide, page 269X).
MARKS: "This is an Original Lingerie Lou Doll" (back)
SEE: *Illustration 188.*
PRICE: $5-10

Dress Me Doll (Lingerie Lou): HP; 7in (17.8cm); see characteristics of the preceding *Lingerie Lou* dolls; face has characteristics of Virga-Beehler Arts dolls; eyes painted and are side glancing; doll dressed in bra and panties of plastic; mohair wig; standard arm hook; one-piece body; jointed at neck and arms only.
MARKS: None; "Lingerie Lou with Removable Plastic Lingerie//A Genuine Plastic Dress-Me Doll//Doll Bodies, Inc. New York 10, N.Y." (box)
SEE: *Illustration 189.* Similar walking doll with plastic bra and panties, (see Plastic Molded Arts, page 207).
PRICE: $5-10

Girl: HP; 7in (17.8cm); *Ginny* look-alike; sleep eyes with molded lashes; dark, painted lashes under eyes; not original outfit; individual fingers; standard arm hook; nonwalker; painted on shoes, (see Identification Guide, page 286K).
MARKS: "A Product of Doll Bodies, Inc., New York, N.Y."
SEE: *Illustration 190. (Louise Schnell Collection.)* See Roberta Doll Co. for other dolls marked "Doll Bodies."
PRICE: $8-15

Illustration 188. *Illustration 189.*

Mary Hartline (Lingerie Lou): HP; 7in (17.8cm); wears the red majorette costume of the famous TV star; white heart and arrow on bodice; white music trim on skirt; 2nd and 3rd fingers molded together; arm hook, (see Identification Guide, page 269X).
MARKS: "This is an Original Creation of Lingerie Lou" (back)
SEE: *Illustration 191. (Pat Parton Collection.)* From left to right: *Lingerie Lou* (Doll Bodies), Ideal's *Mary Hartline.*
PRICE: $15-20

Illustration 190. *Illustration 191.*

DUCHESS DOLL CORPORATION

The Duchess Doll Corporation produced dolls from the late 1940s into the 1950s. The company is best known for their small 7 and 7½in (17.8 and 19.1cm) all hard plastic adult dolls. Several different dolls and faces were used. One had sleep eyes while the other had side glancing painted eyes. The clothes were stapled onto the doll. Both types of dolls had painted, molded shoes. Duchess also made Walt Disney characters and a series called, "Dolls of all Nations." Most of them had Virga type shoes, (see Identification Guide, page 285H); arm hook (see Identification Guide, page 268V).

MARKS: "Duchess Doll Corp.//Design Copyright//1948" (back)

Illustration 192.   *Illustration 193.*

Lady: HP; 7½in (19.1cm); blue side glancing eyes; blue organdy purse and blue felt hat; white organdy dress with blue trim; jointed at arms only; 1st, 2nd, 3rd and 4th fingers molded together.
    MARKS: "Duchess Doll Corp.//Design Copyright//1948."
    SEE: *Illustration 192.*
    PRICE: $15-20

Lady: HP; 7in (17.8cm); blue sleep eyes; jointed at arms and neck; 1st, 2nd, 3rd and 4th fingers molded together; blue dress with pink edging and black lace; matching veil.
    MARKS: "Duchess Doll Corp.//Design Copyright//1948."
    SEE: *Illustration 193.*
    PRICE: $15-20

Illustration 194.

Illustration 195.

Illustration 196.

Tinker Bell: HP; 7in (17.8cm); Walt Disney character; sleep eyes; 1st, 2nd, 3rd and 4th fingers molded together.

   MARKS: "Duchess Doll Corp.//Design Copyright//1948."
   SEE: *Illustration 194. (Beatrice Campbell Collection.)*
   PRICE: $15-20

Martha Washington: HP; 7in (17.8cm); white wig; part of the series "Dolls of all Nations;" in original box; yellow and purple dress with yellow ribbon; white felt hat with yellow ribbon.

   MARKS: "Duchess Doll Corp.//Design Copyright//1948."
   SEE: *Illustration 195. (Marie Ezzo Collection.)*
   PRICE: $15-20

Queen: HP; 7in (17.8cm); part of the series "Dolls of all Nations;" in original box; white and gold dress with a red cape; gold crown; sleep eyes; 1st, 2nd and 3rd fingers molded together.

   MARKS: "Duchess Doll Corp.//Design Copyright//1948."
   SEE: *Illustration 196. (Marie Ezzo Collection.)*
   PRICE: $15-20

EEGEE

E. G. Goldberger founded the company in 1917. While the dolls were made for the mass market, many of the hard plastic dolls are of very good quality. The faces were pretty and the clothes appealed to little girls. The wigs were washable and of excellent quality. The hair style stayed in after washing.

Illustration 197.   *Illustration 198.*   *Illustration 199.*

Little Debutante: vinyl head/arms; HP body/legs; 28in (71.1cm); jointed at elbows and knees; rooted dark blonde hair; blue sleep eyes with lashes and blue eye shadow; pierced ears; high heeled feet; head turning walker; closed mouth; pink satin formal with pink lace overskirt; circa 1958.
MARKS: "20-hh/Eegee" (head)
SEE: *Illustration 197.*
PRICE: $40-45

Susan Stroller: vinyl head; HP body; 17in (43.2cm); pin hipped walker with unpainted pin (see Identification Guide, page 290C); jointed at neck, arms, knees; open/closed mouth with vinyl tongue; sleep eyes with lashes; grill in stomach, (see Identification Guide, page 275B); came in many sizes; distinctive armhook (see Identification Guide, page 263D); individually molded fingers; clothes not original, circa 1957.
MARKS: "EEGEE" (head); "EE-GEE" (body); or none
SEE: *Illustration 198.*
PRICE: $20-30

Merry Stroller: vinyl head; HP body; 13in (33cm); *Saucy Walker* look-alike; sleep eyes with lashes; same doll as *Susan Stroller*; both came in a trunk but with different clothes; closed mouth; painted eyelashes under eyes; pin joint walker with unpainted rivet (see Identification Guide, page 275A); individually molded fingers; not original clothes; armhooks, (see Identification Guide, page 263D); circa 1957.
MARKS: "Eegee" (head)
SEE: *Illustration 199. (Mary Beth Manchook Collection.)*
PRICE: $20-25

DOLLS NOT PHOTOGRAPHED

Eegee made open-mouthed babies with HP heads and latex bodies. They also made a 10½in (26.7cm) chubby girl with a vinyl head and HP body. She was jointed at the knees and was a walker.

An important celebrity doll is *Gigi Perreaux*. She has a vinyl head, HP body, glued on wig and feathered eyebrows. She is marked E.G. on the head. See, Axe, John, "Modern Doll Mysteries, Celebrity Dolls," *Doll Reader,*® October 1983, page 127.

EFFANBEE

Effanbee is a combination of the names of Bernard Fleischaker and Hugo Baum who started making dolls in 1910. They were intrigued with the quality of life in the United States and wanted to let the children of this nation have excellent dolls that were made in the United States.

Their composition dolls are among the most beautiful ever made. By 1946, just as new materials were coming into the doll field, the company was in financial difficulties and was sold to the NOMA Electric Company, and the quality of the dolls deteriorated. In 1953, some of the original members of the firm formed a corporation to buy back the business. The quality then improved. Their hard plastic dolls continued the tradition of beautiful dolls.

The company is still making beautiful dolls, but the official company records of hard plastic dolls are no longer available according to present company officials.

There are excellent books about Effanbee dolls on the market (see Bibliography). Much of the lost information has been reconstructed by these authors.

Honey: 1949-1957

In the 1950s, *Honey* was one of the most popular dolls. She came in a variety of sizes, wigs, flesh tones and costumes. She was well marked with "Effanbee" on the head and back. Most of the flesh tones had an "ivory" quality to them.

Basic *Honey* Characteristics:

They were all hard plastic and had sleep eyes, often brown. There was red coloring on the knees and back of the hands. This doll was jointed at the neck, arms, legs, and had the standard arm joint (see Identification Guide, page 262A).

The wigs were soft and wavy and made of synthetic hair, mohair or human hair. The doll had eyelashes and sleep eyes. Lashes were also painted under the eyes. She had a red dot in the inner corner of each eye.

The individual fingers had dimples under the fingers and the toes had good details but no dimple.

The face is gently rounded with plump cheeks.

The *Honey Walkers*, 1952 to 1957, had the same basic characteristics. The head turns as the doll walks. The neck is longer than the regular *Honeys*. The following illustrations of the *Honey* represent a cross section of the various types and characters produced by Effanbee.

The Honey Doll Series included the following types:
1. Little Girls.
2. Dolls in Formal Attire.
3. Dolls Dressed for Shopping.
4. Bridal Party.
5. School Girls
6. Storybook Characters.
7. Schiaparelli Collection.
8. Ballerinas and Ice Skaters, (see Ballerina and Ice Skater Sections).
9. Majorette.
10. Honey in a Trunk with Extra Clothes.

Illustration 200.

Illustration 201.

Illustration 202.

Illustration 203.

Honey (little girl):   HP; 16in (40.6cm); see *Honey* characteristics (page 88); original purple print dress; light blonde wig; 1949 to 1957.
    MARKS: "Effanbee"
    SEE: *Illustration 200. Illustration 201* (close-up).
    PRICE: $110-130

Prince Charming *(Honey):*   HP; 16in (40.6cm); beautiful blonde wig; feathered eyebrows; pink satin storybook outfit complete with a glass slipper; 1952.
    MARKS: "Effanbee"
    SEE: *Illustration 202.*
    PRICE: $150-185

Alice in Wonderland *(Honey):*   HP; 14in (35.6cm); long blonde hair; blue dress with white pinafore; 1958.
    MARKS: "Effanbee"
    SEE: *Illustration 203. (Emily MacCord Collection.)*
    PRICE: $150-185

Illustration 204.   *Illustration 205.*

Honey: HP; 17½in (44.5cm); pink formal outfit with black velvet neckband; very popular style; circa 1952.

    MARKS: "Effanbee"

    SEE: *Illustration 204. (Barbara Comienski Collection.)*

    PRICE: $130-160

Honey Ballerina: vinyl head; HP body; rooted dark brown hair.

    MARKS: "Effanbee"

    SEE: *Illustration 152* and *Illustration 205.*

    PRICE: $85-110

Dy-Dee Baby: HP head; rubber body and limbs; molded hair or wig; 11in (27.9cm), 15in (38.1cm) and 20in (50.8cm); rubber ears added to head; sometimes wig is caracul; open mouth nurser; 2nd and 3rd fingers molded together; 1950 to 1958. Names for *Dy-Dee* are:

    1. *Dydee Wee* - 9in (22.9cm)

    2. *Dydee Ellen* - 11in (27.9cm)

    3. *Dydee Jane* - 15in (38.1cm)

    4. *Dydee Lu, Lou, Louise* - 20in (50.8cm)

    MARKS: "Effanbee Dy-Dee Baby, U.S. Pat 1859.458; England 380-960; France 723-980; Germany 585-647; Other Pat. Pending."

    PRICE: $75-90

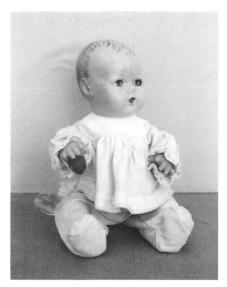

Illustration 206.

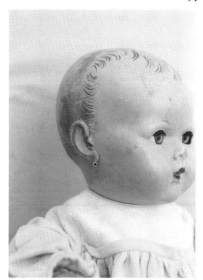

Illustration 207.

Illustration 208.

Illustration 209.

Dy-Dee Baby.
   SEE: *Illustration 206* (clothes not original). *(Phyllis Appell Collection.) Illustration 207* (ear). *(Phyllis Appell Collection.) Illustration 208* (bottle). *(Phyllis Appell Collection.) Illustration 209* (caracul wig). *(Lillian Sakal Collection.)*
   PRICE: $80-90

Illustration 210.

Illustration 211.

Illustration 212.

Illustration 213.

Melodie: vinyl head; HP body; unusually large doll at 27in (68.6cm); jointed knees, talking mechanism; talking; walking; singing; kneeling; praying; turning head; sleep eyes; rooted hair; uses flashlight batteries; original except shoes and socks; pink nylon dress with pink ribbon; straw hat; individual fingers; originally an expensive doll; 1953-1956.

MARKS: "Effanbee" (head)

SEE: *Illustration 210* (doll). *(Barbara Comienski Collection.) Illustration 211.* (tag). *(Barbara Comienski Collection.) Illustration 212* (close-up). *(Barbara Comienski Collection.) Illustration 213* (box). *(Barbara Comienski Collection).*

PRICE: $250-300

Illustration 214.

Illustration 215.

I AM

Mommy's Baby

PRESS MY TUMMY
AND I SAY MOMMY

An
EFFANBEE
WASHABLE LATEX
DOLL

Cuddle me gently in your arms, and I'll
love you and call you "Mommy" like a
real baby. You can bathe me and keep
me clean because my skin is of water-
proof Latex. But — PLEASE! — DO
NOT put my head under water! Then
dry and powder me all over — that
will make me feel so good!
(And because I am an EF-
FANBEE Doll, I'll be
with you for a
long, long
time.)
TRADE MARK REG.
MADE IN
U.S.A.

Illustration 216.

Illustration 217.

Mommy's Baby: HP head and shoulder plate; various sizes; open mouth with two upper teeth; rubber body; individual fingers; original clothes; pink organdy dress and bonnet; white flocked hearts; 1949.

MARKS: None; Golden Heart Label

SEE: *Illustration 214* (doll). *Illustration 215* (face). *Illustration 216* (label). *Illustration 217* (label).

PRICE: $80-100 (if magic skin is in good condition)

Illustration 218.

Mother: vinyl head; HP body; vinyl arms; 20in (50.8cm); walker; jointed knees; high-heel feet; closed mouth; rooted washable hair; red coat with lace collar; cotton print dress; came with family including *Babykins,* sister *Fluffy* and brother *Mickey;* individual fingers; has the same body as the *Jr. Miss Ballerina* (see Ballerina Section); very late, transitional hard plastic; original clothes; 1958.

    MARKS: "EFFANBEE" (head)

    SEE: *Illustration 218.*

    PRICE: $70-90

DOLLS NOT PHOTOGRAPHED:

During the time that the Noma Electric Company owned Effanbee, they produced the *Noma, the Electronic Doll.* She had a HP head and shoulder plate, sleep eyes and brown hair. Her early vinyl arms fit into a metal piece at the shoulders. A battery operated the talking mechanism inside her body. She was 30in (76.2cm) and had an open mouth and two teeth. The Montgomery Ward Catalog of 1950 listed her. She is marked "the Noma Electric Corporation."

Howdy Doody was the first Effanbee HP. He had sleep eyes with molded hair. His body was stuffed. He was produced first in 1947.

In 1954 *Patricia Walker* was listed in the company catalogs. She had a HP body and a vinyl head. She came in various sizes.

Honeykins also was produced in 1954. 12in (30.5cm), she was packed in a hope chest with a large wardrobe of clothes. She is marked "EFF-AN-BEE."

The *Champagne Lady* from the Lawrence Welk Show is a transitional doll produced in 1957. Her head is vinyl and her body is a type of hard plastic. Fully-jointed with an additional joint at the knees, she featured high heeled feet. She was 19in (48.3cm).

EL

Girl: HP; 7in (17.8cm); wearing yellow crocheted dress; Virga type characteristics (see page 240); mitten hands; Virga shoes, (see Identification Guide, page 286J); side-glancing eyes; heavy legs and hips.
MARKS: "El" (body)
SEE: *Illustration 219.*
PRICE: $5-10

Illustration 219.

EUGENIA COMPANY

The Eugenia Company supplied beautiful dolls to Montgomery Ward during the late 1940s and 1950s. The dolls were not marked. Because of the many similarities to the Ideal dolls of the period, it has been suggested that perhaps they were made by Ideal.

Ms. Joanne Calhoun from the sales promotion Ideal staff at CBS Toys, makers of Ideal Dolls, states that she cannot find that Ideal made Eugenia dolls for Montgomery Ward in the early 1950s. They are not listed in the catalogs that she has.

Personality Pla-mate: beautiful HP; 18in (45.7cm); reddish brown hair; feathered eyebrows; sleep eyes with five lines painted at each side of eye; nail polish; 2nd and 3rd fingers molded together and slightly curved; body similar to Nancy Ann *Style Show Doll;* red on knees and hands; wide Y on her seat; mohair wig; pink formal with gold trim; white cotton lace hat; pink flowers; circa 1949. **MARKS:** None

SEE: *Illustration 220* (doll). *Illustration 221* (feathered eyebrow). *Illustration 222* (box).

PRICE: $105-130

Illustration 220.

Illustration 221.

A Personality

Pla-Mate

STYLED FOR
MONTGOMERY WARD
BY EUGENIA DOLL CO.

Illustration 222.

FAIRYLAND DOLLS

Parents enjoyed giving their little girls the beautiful costume dolls for special occasions. The children not only enjoyed them, but they served as a decoration for their room or home.

This company stated that they made, "Famous Figures of Fact and Fancy...Costumed." Many a child still becomes first interested in history and literature through these lovely dolls.

Illustration 223.

Illustration 224.

Irish Girl: HP; 7in (17.8cm); painted side glancing eyes; Virga type basic doll (see Virga); painted shoes, (see Identification Guide, page 284E); white satin skirt with green shamrocks; green bodice; circa 1953.
 MARKS: None; box marked "Fairyland Doll Co."
 SEE: *Illustration 223* (doll). *Illustration 224* (box).
 PRICE: $10-15

FOREIGN HARD PLASTIC

Included in this section are some hard plastic dolls from Europe. These dolls did not develop with the same qualities as those in the United States. However, they do meet the qualifications set forth on pages 4 to 6 in the beginning of the book unless otherwise noted. They are lighter in weight than the American hard plastic doll. Other European companies like Furga, Roddy and Reliable that are more known, are listed under their company name.

Bride: This doll was brought to Pam Judd from Germany in 1955 by her grandmother. It was very much loved by her and the wig is a recent replacement. It does, however, simulate the original. Little girls loved the wonderful, full wigs of the period. The dress is also replaced because as a young girl she spilled green Jello on the original. The doll is painted hard plastic and probably from Italy.

    MARKS: None
    SEE: *Illustration 225.*
    PRICE: Not enough sample prices.

Girl: painted HP; 17in (43.2cm); sleep eyes with lashes; open dome through which can be seen the original sea green color of the plastic; original except for the shoes; white dotted swiss dress with red trim; the company is Fata in Italy.

    MARKS: None on doll; label reads "Fata Milano" on dress
    SEE: *Illustration 226* (doll). *(Pat Parton Collection.) Illustration 227* (dome). *(Pat Parton Collection.)*
    PRICE: $50-60

Girl: HP head; early vinyl body, arms, legs; 18in (45.7cm); marvelous flirty sleep eyes; long lashes; closed mouth; five lash lines painted in corners of eyes; fully-jointed; original clothes; blue gingham jumper; white blouse; purchased in Detroit, Michigan, in 1959.

    MARKS: "Samco, Italy" (manufacturing company)
    SEE: *Illustration 228. (Louise Schnell Collection.)*
    PRICE: Not enough sample prices.

Illustration 225.

Illustration 226.

Illustration 227.

Illustration 228.

Jackie (by Ottolini): painted HP; 25in (63.5cm); flirty, sleep eyes with lashes; heavy eye shadow; closed mouth; molded painted high-heeled shoes; 1st, 2nd and 3rd fingers molded together; painted fingernails; original clothes; two-piece beige dress with beige flowers; purchased in Detroit, Michigan, in 1960.

    MARKS: "Ottolini C & D, Mod Dept., Made in Italy; tag reads "Poupee Originale Ottolini"

    SEE: *Illustration 229. (Louise Schnell Collection.)*

    PRICE: Not enough sample prices.

Illustration 229.   *Illustration 230.*

Lady: painted HP; 25in (63.5cm); flirty, sleep eyes with lashes; heavy eye shadow; closed mouth; molded painted high-heeled shoes; 1st, 2nd and 3rd fingers molded together; painted fingernails; original clothes; rose printed dress; purchased in Detroit, Michigan, in 1960.

    MARKS: "Ottolini C & D, Mod Dept., Made in Italy; tag reads "Poupee Originale Ottolini"

    SEE: *Illustration 230. (Louise Schnell Collection.)*

    PRICE: Not enough sample prices.

Illustration 231.   *Illustration 232.*

German Girl: HP; 12in (30.5cm); sleep eyes with lashes; closed mouth; painted red marks in inner eye and nostrils; 2nd and 3rd fingers molded together; fully-jointed; curly wig; original clothes; provincial costume; green skirt; black vest; white apron. This is a transitional doll which has some celluloid qualities. However, it has all the hard plastic characteristics.

    MARKS: "H & D" (back); "Gura" on tag

    SEE: *Illustration 231.*

    PRICE: $30

Blonde girl: HP; 23in (53.4cm); enormous mohair wig; sleep eyes with long lashes; fully-jointed; ruffled red dress trimmed in white lace.

    MARKS: None

    SEE: *Illustration 232. (Pat Parton Collection.)*

    PRICE: $80-90

FORTUNE DOLL COMPANY

In the 1950s beauty was important to women. They wore heavy makeup, especially lipstick. Clothes were very feminine. The dolls of the period reflected the culture current at the time.

The Fortune Doll Company marketed thousands of dolls in connection with Beehler Arts and Ontario Plastics. There were big differences in quality, but all were pretty, feminine and the lips were bright red. Their dolls have beautiful eyes emphasizing the eye itself rather than eye shadow. The pupils were deep blue or black, and the surrounding eye sparkled. One unusually well-made doll had simulated paperweight eyes that followed the viewer.

The company competed with *Ginny* and *Ginger,* calling their doll *Pam.* Her characteristics are the same as *Lucy* (see Virga), which was also a product of Beehler Art.

Another small walking doll was *Ninette* which was previewed at the Toy Fair in 1955. She was 8in (20.3cm) and moved her head as she walked. She had 24 extra outfits and had the same characteristics as *Pam* and *Lucy*. The doll retailed for $1.98, and the dresses were $.98.

Their larger dolls, about 12in (30.5cm), often had a felt circle on their hair, stapled to a bonnet shape.

Illustration 233.　　　　　　　*Illustration 234.*

Pam:　HP; 8in (20.3cm); walkers and nonwalkers; head turns on walkers; long rather stocky body; molded T-strap shoes, painted or unpainted; crease in center of knee; seam runs behind back section of ear; sometimes molded hair under wig; deep indentation under lower lip, no dimple like *Ginger*; 2nd and 3rd fingers molded together; distinctive arm joint which makes identification easy if original arms are on doll, (see Identification Guide, page 2660); knees not jointed; sleep eyes with molded lashes; closed mouth; *Pam* was used for the Fab advertising doll; circa 1955.

MARKS: None

SEE: *Illustration 233* (walker). Orange coat and hat; white dress with orange and blue print. *Illustration 234* (purple wig). Purple dress; white lace trim and sleeves. *(Barbara Comienski Collection.)*

PRICE: $15-25

Illustration 235. *Illustration 236A.* *Illustration 236B.*

Illustration 237. *Illustration 238.*

Pam Ballerina: HP; (see description of *Pam*); only difference is that the feet are pointed like a ballerina. Pink tutu and ballet shoes; circa 1955.

> **MARKS:** None; box reads: "Michele Cartier presents Pam and her Fabulous Wardrobe; Fortune Toy, Inc., Jackson Heights, N.Y.;" top of box reads: "My name is Pam, A pretty doll, I stand up, I sit down, I also walk around and around."
> **SEE:** *Illustration 235. (Laura Brown Collection.)*
> **PRICE:** $30-40

Girl: HP; 9in (22.9cm); sleep eyes with molded lashes; arched eyebrows; no molded-on shoes; tube arm hook (see Identification Guide, page 266O); individual fingers; knees have two dimples; head turning walker; purple costume with pink sash; straw hat.

> **MARKS:** None
> **SEE:** *Illustration 236A. (Pat Parton Collection.) Illustration 236B* (knees).
> **PRICE:** $15-20

"Blue Ribbon Classics:" *The Heart Throb Doll with a Heart Beat;* **Bridesmaid:** HP; 12in (30.5cm); nonwalker; sleep eyes with molded lashes; simulated paperweight eyes that follow the viewer and shine brightly; delicately arched eyebrows; beautiful bisque-like quality of the hard plastic; body of lesser quality; molded, painted Virga-type shoes (see Identification Guide, page 285G); high pointed mouth; eyelashes painted under eyes; beautiful long, slim fingers with 1st, 2nd, 3rd, 4th fingers molded together; wrist line on palm side only; quality mohair wig; single line seat (see Identification Guide, page 282C); prominent joining seams over entire body; closed

Illustration 239.

Illustration 240.

Illustration 241.

mouth; stapled onto the stomach is a satin pouch with a mechanism which simulates a heart beat. It operates when the doll is moved or carried; pink satin dress; blue felt hat.

MARKS: None; box labels "Blue Ribbon Classics, Fortune Toy, Inc., Brooklyn, N.Y."

SEE: *Illustration 237. (Ann Pendleton Collection.) Illustration 238* (close-up). *(Ann Pendleton Collection.)*

PRICE: $20-35

Unmarked with Fortune Characteristics

Girl: HP; 12in (30.5cm); head turning walker; poor quality HP; sleep eyes with deep blue centers and crystal-like outer edges; 2nd and 3rd fingers molded together; wrist line on palm side only; deep red lips with Fortune characteristics; single line on seat (see Identification Guide, page 282C); red mohair wig; purple bodice with yellow skirt; stapled-on purple felt circle hat; closed mouth. Often seen in Admiration Co. boxes.

MARKS: None

SEE: *Illustration 239.*

PRICE: $8-15.

Violetta: shiny HP; 12in (30.5cm); sleep eyes with lashes; large dark pupils; delicately arched eyebrows; 1st, 2nd and 3rd fingers molded together; wrist line on palm side of hand only; brown mohair wig with felt circle hat; hat and feathers stapled on head; molded, painted Virga-type shoes with no bows (see Identification Guide, page 285I); one line on seat (see Identification Guide, page 282C); painted lips; arm hook (see Identification Guide, page 267S).

MARKS: None; tag reads: "Violetta from the Opera La Traviata by Verdi." The story of the opera is inside.

SEE: *Illustration 240. Illustration 241.*

PRICE: $15-25

G. H. & E. FREYDBERG, INC.

Mary Jane: HP; 17in (43.2cm); made in imitation of *Terri Lee;* closed mouth that is wider than *Terri Lee;* flirty eyes; eyebrows more arched than *Terri Lee;* painted eyelashes on side of eye; redder flesh color and more glossy than *Terri Lee;* head turns as it walks; 2nd and 3rd fingers molded together; more slender body than *Terri Lee;* sleep eyes; 30 outfits available; 1955.

MARKS: None

SEE: *Illustration 242 (Mary Jane* in green pajamas). *Illustration 243 (Mary Jane* in plaid jumper). *(Pat Parton Collection.)*

PRICE: $150-175

Illustration 242.   *Illustration 243.*

FURGA

Furga is one of the largest doll manufacturing companies in the world. The company is located in the center of Northern Italy in Lombardy. It was established in the 1870s. Over the years, many different types of dolls have been made and after World War II, they were one of the first in Europe to use a type of hard plastic. This plastic was somewhat different from the hard plastic which was emerging in the United States.

Girl: European lightweight hard plastic; painted; 11½in (29.2cm); fluttery eyes that sparkle; fully-jointed; pointed fingers with nail polish; 2nd and 3rd fingers molded together; cryer grid in back; closed mouth; brown wig; wearing yellow organdy dress; white collar.

MARKS: "Furga, Italy"

SEE: *Illustration 244. (Heloise Miles Collection.)*

PRICE: $35

Illustration 244.

HALCO

DOLLS NOT PHOTOGRAPHED

Halco made a *Miss Fluffie* doll; 29in (73.7cm); HP head, cloth body, latex limbs; open mouth. She is unmarked.

HOLLYWOOD

Hollywood made many different kinds of dolls during its years in business. They were often small, inexpensive, unmarked or marked dolls made for the mass market.

Most of the dolls available to collectors are the composition or bisque type. An example is the "Mayfair Birthstone Dolls." They also produced hard plastic dolls, but they are much rarer than their other dolls. Hard plastic dolls were manufactured in the late 1940s into the early 1950s.

Girl: HP; 5½in (14cm); painted eyes looking upward; molded hair under wig; swivel head; protruding lower stomach; 1st, 2nd, 3rd and 4th fingers molded together; circa 1950.
MARKS: Star "Hollywood Doll" (back)
SEE: *Illustration 245. (Lillian Sakal Collection.)*
PRICE: $5-7

Baby in buggy: HP; 4½in (11.5cm); jointed head; original clothes and buggy; circa late 1940s to early 1950s.
MARKS: Star "Hollywood Dolls" (back)
SEE: *Illustration 246. (Helen Kirschnick Collection.)*
PRICE: $20-30

Illustration 245. *Illustration 246.*

HORSMAN

A true pioneer in producing the modern indestructible doll, the E. T. Horsman Company started making composition "Can't Break Em" dolls in small quantities before 1912. Their dolls were unusual, comical, beautiful, lovable and very collectible.

According to Ruth Freeman in her *Cavalcade of Dolls A Basic Book*, page 231, Horsman has the credit for introducing Plastisol Dolls (a type of hard plastic) into the toy market in 1946.

Today many of the marked and unmarked open mouth dolls, as well as some closed mouth dolls, are found at doll shows, antique stores and flea markets. They have a distinctive face and can easily be identified with practice.

True to the dream of the founders of the Horsman Company, many are in excellent condition. They may have lost their original clothes but they clean up beautifully. Their unusual sparkling eyes still light up the hearts of doll lovers of all ages.

MARKS: Many are unmarked

160
170 seems to be 15 to 16in (38.1 to 40.6cm)
180 seems to be 18in (45.7cm)
Horsman Company
Horsman
Series of dots / Horsman
Made in U.S.A.

GENERAL CHARACTERISTICS OF HORSMAN ALL-HARD PLASTIC DOLLS

1. Marked and unmarked.
2. Crystal-like bright eyes.
3. Individual fingers with 2nd and 3rd curved inward.
4. Open mouth with four teeth.
5. Felt tongue.
6. Horsman arm joint with bar across on walkers.
7. Unusually large indentation (roundish) under nose.
8. Dimples on back of hand.
9. Wrist line around entire wrist.
*10. Painted inset pins on pin jointed walking mechanism (sometimes paint has chipped off, but there is usually some indication of paint). (See Identification Guide, page 290A).
11. Sometimes ᵒᵧᵒ on seat - non walkers (see illustration, page 282B).
12. Sometimes a diamond shape on backside (see illustration, page 282A).
13. Walkers have only "Y" on seat.
14. Knees and wrists painted red; sometimes it is worn off.
15. There are two types of bodies; 1. mature and slim; 2. the chunkier little girl type.
16. Flesh tones vary from a whitish tone to a pretty tan. Quality of the plastic varies more than with other companies. Some dolls are excellent quality and some are poor.

17. Standard arm on nonwalker (see Identification Guide, page 266P or 267Q, No. 17).
18. Some dolls have standard walking arms. Others have walker arms which prohibit dolls from raising their arms above their heads.
19. Head turns on walkers.
*Important identifying factor.

Illustration 247.   *Illustration 248.*

Cindy: HP; various sizes; crystal-like glass eyes; individual fingers; standard arm hook on nonwalkers; standard walker type hook on walkers; early dolls had hip pin walker with painted pin joints; others had standard walking mechanism; early dolls had two holes in the head which were supposed to hold the walking mechanism; open mouth; four teeth; felt tongue; some were closed mouth or open/closed mouth.

This doll was made in two distinct types:
1. The child doll with a child's shape.
2. Teen girl with a slimmer body.

There is a big difference in the quality of the plastic used. The early ones were painted hard plastic. Later ones were made of a plastic with the flesh tone added before the doll was put in the mold; 1950 to 1955.

MARKS: "Horsman; 160, 170, 180; Made in U.S.A." (body); or none

Girl *(Cindy):* HP; slim teen figure; 17½in (44.5cm); nonwalker; painted HP; Horsman individual fingers, open mouth; four teeth; felt tongue; sleep crystal-like eyes; eyelashes; clothes may not be original; circa 1950.
MARKS: None
SEE: *Illustration 247. (Pat Parton Collection.)*
PRICE: $45-55

Girl *(Cindy):* HP; slim figure; 18in (45.7cm); yellow jumper with a white blouse; braided mohair wig; sleep crystal-like eyes; felt tongue; four teeth; arms can be raised only to shoulder; standard Horsman hand; pin jointed walker with countersunk painted pin (see Identification Guide, page 290A); circa 1952.
MARKS: "Horsman 180"
SEE: *Illustration 248. (Pat Parton Collection.)*
PRICE: $45-55

Illustration 249.

Illustration 250.

Illustration 251.

Illustration 252.

Girl Roller Skater: painted HP; slim type; open mouth; four teeth and felt tongue; sleep crystal-like eyes with lashes; painted lashes under eyes; walker; arm hook, (see Identification Guide, page 263E); arms raised only shoulder high; not in original clothes; circa 1952.

> **MARKS:** None
> **SEE:** *Illustration 249. (Pat Parton Collection.)*
> **PRICE:** $35-45

Girl *(Cindy):* HP; 16in (40.6cm); child type; original clothes; crystal-like eyes; open mouth with four teeth and felt tongue; Horsman arm hook (see Identification Guide, page 266P); Horsman hands; painted eyelashes below eyes; head turning walker; original clothes pink organdy; pink sash flowers; circa 1952.

> **MARKS:** "170" (back)
> **SEE:** *Illustration 250. (Phyllis Appell Collection.)*
> **PRICE:** $60-85

Girl *(Cindy):* HP; teen type; 17½in (44.5cm); pin jointed walker with painted pin; blonde mohair wig; Horsman hand; crystal-like sleep eyes; painted eyelashes below eyes; open mouth with four teeth; felt tongue; walker holes in head under wig; original blue formal clothes; replaced flowers.

> **MARKS:** None
> **SEE:** *Illustration 251.*
> **PRICE:** $45-55

Lu Ann Simms *(Cindy):* HP; teen type; 18in (45.7cm); open mouth with four teeth and felt tongue; pin jointed walker with painted pins; individual fingers; long brunette wig with upswept hair in front and full in back; blue eyes; yellow piqué dress; green rickrack trim; circa 1953.

> **MARKS:** "Horsman 180" (neck); or "Made in USA/170" (body)
> **SEE:** *Illustration 252.*
> **PRICE:** $55-75

Comparison Illustration: _____

Horsman made many dolls for other companies. Often the collector will find Mollye, Valentine and other dolls with Horsman traits.

In *Illustration 253* all three dolls look alike; circa 1953. The doll on the right is a *Lu Ann Simms* doll, and the doll on the left is an identical Horsman with a different wig and clothes. The doll in the middle is a *Lu Ann Simms* by Valentine. Both the taller 18in (45.7cm) dolls have the mark: Horsman 180. The smaller doll, by Valentine, has the marks: Made in U.S.A. Pat. Pending, on the back. The larger dolls have blue eyes and the smaller doll has brown eyes. Costumes - right: yellow piqué dress with green rickrack trim; middle: blue print dress with white yoke and sleeves; left: yellow jumper with white blouse.

Both *Lu Ann Simms* dolls have the same styled wig; the 18in (45.7cm) *Lu Ann Simms* has also been used with a Roberta wrist label and a "180" marking without the Horsman.

This is another example of the interaction of doll companies during the 1950s.

SEE: *Illustration 253. (Pat Parton Collection.)*

Illustration 253.   *Illustration 254.*   *Illustration 255.*

Gretel: vinyl head; HP body; 14in (35.6cm); rooted hair; caricature from Walt Disney movie; *Hansel* and *Gretel* have the same face and body, but different hair and costumes; vinyl face is "sticky" early vinyl; hip pin walker with painted countersunk pin; head turns when walking; reproduction of Kinemins in movie; sleep eyes with lashes; closed mouth; four fingers molded together; all original blue and white striped cotton dress; white organdy apron; red rickrack trim; red shoes; early 1950s.

MARKS: "Made in U.S.A." (circle on body); tag on doll

SEE: *Illustration 254 (Gretel* only).

PRICE: $100-125

Mama Doll: painted HP head with rubber "magic skin" type body; 18½in (47cm); sleep eyes with lashes; closed mouth; beautiful flesh tone; mohair wig; blue dress; white lace trim; early 1950s.

MARKS: "Horsman" (head)

SEE: *Illustration 255* (doll). *Illustration 256* (close-up page 110).

PRICE: $25-30

Illustration 256.

Illustration 257.

Illustration 258.

UNKNOWN DOLL WITH HORSMAN CHARACTERISTICS

Saucy Walker-type: HP; 23in (58.4cm); sleep eyes with lashes; open mouth with four teeth; individual fingers; grill on stomach, hip pin walker with countersunk, painted pin (see Identification Guide, page 290A); diamond seat; original clothes; pink dress and matching bonnet trimmed in pink flowered print; circa 1951.

MARKS: None
SEE: *Illustration 257. (Pat Parton Collection.)*
PRICE: $45-60

Saucy Walker-type: vinyl head; HP; 19½in (49.6cm); head turning walker; grid on stomach (see Identification Guide, page 275C); two faint "o's" above the diamond seat; dimples over toes and under fingers; sleep eyes with lashes; lashes painted under eyes; two lines at inner fold of elbow; wrist lines around entire doll.

MARKS: "31 AE"
SEE: *Illustration 258. (Pat Parton Collection.)*
PRICE: $35-50

DOLLS NOT PHOTOGRAPHED

Horsman produced HP girl dolls under various names such as *Bright Star, Cindy Kay* and *Dolly Dreamland.*

HOSELEY PARTY DOLLS
(McGregor, Iowa)

Hoseley Party Dolls made a series of miniature ladies in 56 different costumes. They were HP 15in (38.1cm) with various pretty hair styles, circa 1954 to 1955.

MARY HOYER

Mary Hoyer had a yarn shop in Reading, Pennsylvania, and sold many types of yarn and other craft supplies through a mail order business. She conceived the idea of a lovely doll which could be sold to customers along with pattern books and instructions for knitting and crocheting clothes. Most of the dolls were sold without clothes. Many church and philanthropic groups purchased these dolls and sold them for money making projects.

The patterns were intricate and lovely. Today the majority of Mary Hoyer dolls have some of these handmade outfits.

However, Mrs. Hoyer did have some garments made in her workrooms and many of these doll clothes were labeled. She also sold some accessories such as shoes, skates, school bags, wigs, wave sets, trunks, parasols, fur capes, head bands and others.

Identification Hints:

Mary Hoyer's recently published book, *Mary Hoyer and Her Dolls* (Hobby House Press, Inc.), shows pictures of the various costumes, both handmade and professionally made. They will help identify the doll.

Many collectors do not buy the boy doll because they mistakenly believe that someone has cut off his hair. Brother has either a fur wig or a regular wig with a ragged cut. This is the way it was sold.

Girl: HP; 14in (35.6cm); glass-like sleep eyes; closed mouth; wig; 2nd and 3rd fingers slightly curled; pointed chin; tiny face in comparison with other hard plastic dolls; beautiful porcelain-like skin color; standard arms; jointed in neck, arms, legs; real lashes and lashes painted under eyes; late 1940s to early 1950s.

MARKS: "The Mary Hoyer Doll;" or (in circle) "Original Mary Hoyer Doll"
SEE: *Illustration 259.* (doll). *Illustration 260* (close-up). *Illustration 261.* (*McCall's Needlework Magazine,* Fall-Winter 1953-1954). *(Pat Parton Collection.)*
PRICE: $150-200

Illustration 259.

Illustration 260.

Illustration 261.

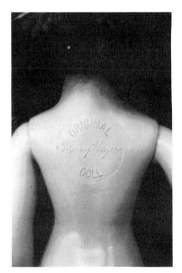

Illustration 263.

Illustration 262.

Boy: HP; 14in (35.6cm); (see description of Mary Hoyer girl); ragged auburn wig haircut; red plaid shirt and jeans; early 1950s.

    MARKS: "The Mary Hoyer Doll;" or (in circle) "Original Mary Hoyer Doll"

    SEE: *Illustration 262. (Helen Kirschnick Collection.) Illustration 263* (close-up of mark).

    PRICE: $150-200

PEGGY HUFFMAN ORIGINAL

There were many individuals, as well as well-known manufacturers, who created whole lines of pretty dolls. This is one example. The maker purchased dolls in quantity. They are very similar to the priest doll in the *Marcie* line, (see A & H).

Illustration 264.

Illustration 266.

Illustration 265.

Illustration 267.

Miss Valentine: HP; 7in (17.8cm); same characteristics as *Queen Isabella*; red skirt with white apron trimmed in red lace.

    MARKS: None on body; tag on dress "February 1956//Miss Valentine Doll of the Month//A Peggy Huffman Original//Reg. Trademark Jefferson City, Mo."

    SEE: *Illustration 264. (Dolly Jakubecz Collection.) Illustration 265* (tag).

    PRICE: $10-15

Queen Isabella of Spain: HP; 7in (17.8cm); jointed at arms and neck; PMA characteristics; three lines for bow on black painted feet (see Identification Guide, page 283B); two lines in palm of hand; mohair wig; sleep eyes; painted eyelashes above eyes; molded fingers at bottom, but separate at top; pink dress with flowered trim.

    MARKS: Tag on dress "Peggy Huffman Original//October 1956//Doll of the Month//Queen Isabella of Spain//Reg. trademark Jefferson City, Mo."

    SEE: *Illustration 266. Illustration 267* (tag).

    PRICE: $10-15

Illustration 268.

Illustration 270.

NOVEMBER 1958
DOLL OF THE MONTH
Pryangtisvasti, from THAILAND
A Peggy Huffman original
Jefferson City, Mo.

APRIL, 1956
EASTER SUNSHINE
DOLL OF THE MONTH
A Peggy Huffman original
Reg. Trademark
Jefferson City, Mo.

Illustration 269.   *Illustration 271.*

Pryangtisvasti: HP; 7in (17.8cm); same characteristics as *Queen Isabella.*
    MARKS: Tag on dress "November 1958//Doll of the Month//Pryangtisvasti
    from Thailand//A Peggy Huffman Original Jefferson City, Mo."
    SEE: *Illustration 268. (Dolly Jakubecz Collection.) Illustration 269* (tag). *(Dolly
    Jakubecz Collection.)*
    PRICE: $10-15

Easter Sunshine: HP; 7in (17.8cm); same characteristics as *Queen Isabella;* yellow
dress and hat with black trim; carrying a daisy.
    MARKS: Tag on dress "April 1956//Easter Sunshine Doll of the Month//A
    Peggy Huffman Original//Reg. Trademark Jefferson City, Mo."
    SEE: *Illustration 270. Illustration 271* (tag).
    PRICE: $10-15

ICE SKATING QUEENS

Ice skating started in northern Europe as a means of transportation. It later became a sport for men, women and children. In 1924 a chubby, sunny blonde child of eleven appeared in the Winter Olympic Games in Chamonix, France, and changed the sport for women. Sonja Henie won both hearts and gold medals, and beautiful dolls reflected her graceful charm.

In 1947 and 1948, Barbara Ann Scott of Canada was world champion. Both amateur skaters turned professional and ice reviews became wonderful theatrical entertainment.

Little girls donned the short skirts and white skates they had seen in the movies and at the coliseums and took lessons. They dreamed of an Olympic or professional career, and they asked for skating costumes for *Terri Lee, Ginny, Ginger* and other hard plastic dolls. Mary Hoyer sent instructions for crocheting or knitting outfits for her lovely dolls through her wide mail order business.

An early hard plastic skating doll made by Madame Alexander was almost an exact copy of the composition *Sonja*. Her name was *Babs*. Additional ice costumes could be purchased for her.

The world of this era loved glitter and beautiful clothes. Ice skaters captured this world, and the dolls of the period were graceful and beautiful.

Babs Skater: early HP; by Madame Alexander; 18in (45.7cm). She is almost an exact copy of the composition *Sonja*. She came in several different costumes; this doll is wearing a pink outfit with matching hat; pink marabou trim; gold skates; 1949.

MARKS: "ALEX" (head); (dress tab) "Babs Skating"//Madame Alexander, N.Y., U.S.A.//All Rights Reserved."
SEE: *Illustration 272.*
PRICE: $350-400

Illustration 272.

Illustration 274.

Illustration 273.

Terri Lee: Another hard plastic doll made from the new plastic materials perfected in World War II was *Terri Lee*. Little girls and their mothers, too, loved the beautiful, expensive wardrobe for this wonderful doll. The glittering pink original costume including hat was decorated with red hearts and cost $16.95 for both the doll and outfit; circa late 1940s; silver skates.

Illustration 275.

> **MARKS:** "Terri Lee Pat. Pending;" tagged outfit
> **SEE:** *Illustration 273.*
> **PRICE:** $150-175 (in this costume)

Cindy: HP; by Horsman. This charmer has a beautiful light-colored skin tone; original costume was woven flannel-type material with red corduroy trim; matching hat; circa 1950 to 1955.

> **MARKS:** "Horsman" (head)
> **SEE:** *Illustration 274. (Pat Parton Collection.)*
> **PRICE:** $50-75

Nannette: HP; by Arranbee. This company dressed a hard plastic doll in a gold felt skirt and knitted white and gold sweater. Like little girls everywhere, her ankles seem a little weak; 1952 to 1955.

> **MARKS:** "R & B" (head)
> **SEE:** *Illustration 275. (Pat Parton Collection.)*
> **PRICE:** $85-110; more for larger sizes

Illustration 276.

Illustration 278.

Illustration 277.

Nannette: HP; 14in (35.6cm) by Arranbee. During the 1950s, separate ice skates could be purchased. These skates complimented a typical dress of the period; green striped dress; red sweater; 1952 to 1955.

    MARKS: "R & B" (head)
    SEE: *Illustration 276. (Pat Parton Collection.)*
    PRICE: $75-90

Mary Hoyer: HP; 14in (35.6cm). A very famous costume for doll ice skaters was the blue crocheted costume including hat designed by Mary Hoyer. She had a knitting store and mail order company in Reading, Pennsylvania. She sent patterns and yarn to customers. Her patterns for dolls have become famous. Late 1940s to early 1950s.

    MARKS: "The Mary Hoyer Doll;" or (in circle) "Original Mary Hoyer Doll"
    SEE: *Illustration 277. (Laura Brown Collection.)*
    PRICE: $125-175

Li'l Imp: vinyl head; HP body; by Vogue; 10½in (26.7cm); red outfit including hat with white trim. This *Li'l Imp* is not quite steady on her feet. She is a later doll from about 1959.

    MARKS: "R & B" (head)
    SEE: *Illustration 278. (Barbara Comienski Collection.)*
    PRICE: $35-45

Illustration 279.   *Illustration 280.*   *Illustration 281.*

Girl: HP; 14in (35.6cm); unknown manufacturer. A mystery is this lovely doll with a homemade dress. Some little girl loved her very much.

    MARKS: "14" (head); "Made in U.S.A." (back)

    SEE: *Illustration 279. (Barbara Comienski Collection.)*

    PRICE: $40-50

Ginny: HP; 7½in (19.1cm); by Vogue. *Ginny* steps out jauntily with a red dress trimmed with white fur. She has sleep eyes with painted lashes and straight legs. 1950 to 1954.

    MARKS: "Vogue" (head); "Ginny Vogue Dolls, Inc. Pat #2687594 Made in U.S.A." (body)

    SEE: *Illustration 280. (Jackie Kaner Collection.)*

    PRICE: $170-200

Ginger: HP; 7½in (19.1cm); by Cosmopolitan. *Ginger, Ginny's* competitor, also steps out in a similar red and white costume; circa 1954.

    MARKS: None

    SEE: *Illustration 281. (Pat Parton Collection.)*

    PRICE: $35-45

Ice Follies Dolls

Right after World War II, Olympic and World Champion skaters turned professional following in the footsteps of Sonja Henie, and the great ice shows were established as theatrical entertainment.

Shipstead and Johnson created their famous Ice Follies and spent millions of dollars on costumes. At the end of each show there was a gorgeous production with outstanding costumes. As the audiences left the shows with the beautiful skaters and wonderful music still vivid in their memory, vendors displayed a 7½in (19.1cm) fashion doll in a copy of the finale costume.

Illustration 282.   *Illustration 283.*

Illustration 284.

Illustration 285.

Anna Barile's husband bought her one each year until they were no longer available. These dolls are brilliant in color and greatly beloved by their owners.

Only some of them have been identified by year. All are hard plastic and have Plastic Molded Arts Characteristics except the 1956 doll, which is marked: "Knickerbocker."

No prices are given because of rarity and lack of price samples.

MARKS: None except the one doll marked "Knickerbocker"

Skater: HP; by Ice Follies; doll in purple celluloid type of material. All of these dolls came in plastic see-through containers; 1956.
   MARKS: "Knickerbocker"
   SEE: *Illustration 282. (Anna Barile Collection.)*

Skater: HP; by Ice Follies; pure white graced an ice queen as the audience cheered.
   SEE: *Illustration 283. (Anna Barile Collection.)*

Skater: HP; by Ice Follies; bright red dress with a white collar was a spectacular costume for a brilliant end.
   SEE: *Illustration 284. (Anna Barile Collection.)*

Skater: HP; by Ice Follies; a blue skirt and silver top with a bright magenta bow was a showstopper.
   SEE: *Illustration 285. (Anna Barile Collection.)*

Illustration 286.   Illustration 287.   Illustration 288.

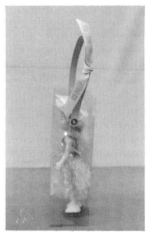

Illustration 289.   Illustration 290.

Skater: HP; by Ice Follies; pink with silver glitter sprinkled throughout the costume encouraged the cheers of the crowd; 1960.

SEE: *Illustration 286. (Anna Barile Collection.)*

Skater: HP; by Ice Follies; a daring, short blue costume with a huge feather plume in the hair was the vision taken away by the audience this year; 1961.

SEE: *Illustration 287. (Anna Barile Collection.)*

Skater: HP; by Ice Follies; another red dazzle costume with a red feather plume in the hair was spectacular from the audience.

SEE: *Illustration 288. (Anna Barile Collection.)*

Skater: HP; by Ice Follies; a long transparent dress of "white ice" was a graceful conclusion during the final number. The plastic box had the Shipstead and Johnson label on the handle; 1963.

SEE: *Illustration 289. (Anna Barile Collection.) Illustration 290* (box). *(Anna Barile Collection.)*

Illustration 292.

Illustration 291.

Illustration 293.

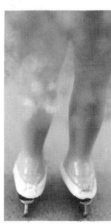

Illustration 294.

Skater: HP; by Ice Follies. The bagpipes swirled as the colorful Scotch lassies skated onto the ice; red and black plaid outfit; 1964.

    SEE: *Illustration 291. (Anna Barile Collection.)*

Skater: HP; by Ice Follies. A change of scene brought the audience a happy conclusion with this white and black strapless costume.

    SEE: *Illustration 292. (Anna Barile Collection.)*

Skater: HP; by Ice Follies. In this year the audience loved the glittery blue and silver skating dress with a large flower at the neckline; 1968.

    SEE: *Illustration 293. (Anna Barile Collection.)*

    The final illustration shows a pair of ice skates attached to a typical A&H shoe (see Identification Guide, page 284D). By 1968, the era of hard plastic dolls had been over for many years, and the dolls were no longer sold. The audiences and Anna missed the tiny souvenirs.

    SEE: *Illustration 294. (Anna Barile Collection.)*

IDEAL

In 1903, Theodore Roosevelt went hunting for bears in Mississippi. A frightened bear cub stumbled into camp, but the President would not shoot it. A Washington newspaper cartoonist, Clifford Berryman, drew a cartoon about the incident. Morris Michtom, owner of a small stationery and novelty store in Brooklyn, New York, had his wife make a pair of stuffed bears by hand for a window display along with the cartoon.

Both bears were purchased the same day, and Mr. Michtom sent a sample to "Teddy" asking permission to name the bear cub after him. The President answered in a hand-written note; "I doubt if my name will mean much in the bear business, but you may use it if you wish." He signed it with the famous "T.R."

Soon the demand for Teddy Bears was so great that the manufacturers could hardly keep up with the orders. The Ideal Company was off to a tremendous start.

Ideal Toy Company was a leader in the industry from its beginning. Immediately after World War II, they used their creativity to start a new line of dolls using nylon, vinyl, acrylics and other plastics which were immediately best sellers.

They advertised widely in *Ladies Home Journal, This Week, Saturday Evening Post, Farm Journal, Progressive Farmer* and the Sunday newspaper's supplement.

MARKS: Ideal's patent for hard plastic is 2252077.

"Ideal Doll/ Made in U.S.A."

"16// Ideal Doll// Made in U.S.A."

"Made in U.S.A., Pat. #2252077."

"Ideal"

"Ideal Doll VP 17 or 23 (head or back)"

"Ideal W 16"

"P 50 Ideal// Made in U.S.A."

"P 90 or P 91 or P 92 or P 93"

"McCall Corp (with) P 90"

"Ideal Doll// 9"

"P 200"

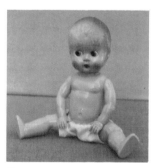

Illustration 295.

Baby: HP; 8in (20.3cm); side glancing eyes.

> **MARKS:** "Ideal" (back)
> **SEE:** *Illustration 295. (Pat Parton Collection.)*
> **PRICE:** $10-16

Baby: HP; 12in (30.5cm); side glancing eyes; painted eyes; fully-jointed; molded hair.

> **MARKS:** "Ideal"
> **SEE:** *Illustration 296. (Rosemary Romance Collection.)*
> **PRICE:** $15-25

Illustration 296.

Illustration 297.

"Original Ideal Catalog not available for better photograph."

Illustration 298.

***Honeysuckle* Babies:** HP; 12in (30.5cm); rubber body, arms, legs; sleep eyes; "She sleeps, wets, drinks from her bottle, she can be bathed and powdered like a real baby;" came in black version; 1949 to 1950.

    MARKS: Unknown

    SEE: *Illustration 297* (page 10, Ideal's Doll Catalog, 1949-50).

    PRICE: $40-50

Magic-Squeezee Babies: HP head; cotton stuffed body; had three voices; one in body and other two in legs; magic skin arms and legs; 16in (40.6cm), 18in (45.7cm) and 20in (50.8cm); molded hair or mohair wig; 1949-1950.

    MARKS: "Ideal Doll, Made in U.S.A."

    SEE: *Illustration 298* (page 14, Ideal's Doll Catalog 1949-50).

    PRICE: $40-50

Illustration 299.

Illustration 300.

Musical Doll Baby: HP head; stuffed cotton body; latex arms and legs; 17in (43.2cm); Swiss music box in body; 1949 to 1950.

MARKS: Unknown

SEE: *Illustration 299* (page TD14, Ideal's Doll Catalog, 1951).

PRICE: Not enough price samples available

Sparkle Plenty (baby): Ideal used comic characters quite often. Dick Tracy was one of the most popular cartoons of the period, and the imagination of the world was aroused when B.O. Plenty and Gravel Gertie were "expecting." Millions wondered what the artist, Chester Gould, would create. Instead of the peculiar features of the parents, little Sparkle was beautiful. Ideal's new doll with long, blonde hair was an immediate success; circa 1947.

HP head with magic skin body; closed mouth; long blonde wig; jointed arms and legs; sleep eyes with eyelashes; 14in (35.6cm) and 18in (45.7cm). The company advertised that she could be washed, bathed and powdered like a real baby. She was dressed in overalls and packed in a full color box illustrating the Dick Tracy comic strip. *Sparkle Plenty* cries or coos depending upon how hard you squeeze her.

MARKS: "Made in USA, Pat #2232077"

SEE: *Illustration 300* (page TD10, Ideal's Doll Catalog, 1951).

PRICE: $40-50

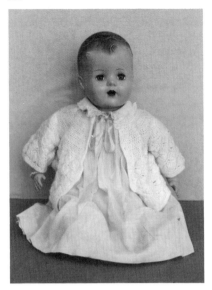

Illustration 301.

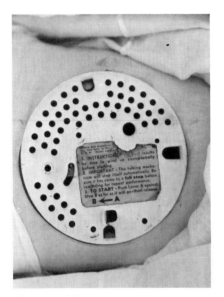

Illustration 302.

Talking Tot: HP head; cloth and vinyl; 22in (55.9cm); wig over molded hair; sleep eyes; key wind talker; laughs when laying down; cries otherwise; 1950.
MARKS: None
SEE: *Illustration 301. (Phyllis Appell Collection.)*
       Illustration 302 key wind talker. *(Phyllis Appell Collection.)*
PRICE: $65-70 (in working condition)

Tickletoes (baby): HP head and shoulder plate; latex arms and legs; 15in (38.1cm); 17in (43.2cm); 19in (48.3cm); 21in (53.3cm); sleep eyes; open mouth with two teeth and tongue except in the 15in (38.1cm) size; glass sleep eyes; molded hair; some had magic skin; some had a wig; some had cotton body; lifelike crying voice.
MARKS: "16/Ideal Doll Made in USA" (head); "P2000 Ideal Doll" (head)
SEE: *Illustration 303* (page TD10, Ideal's Doll Catalog, 1951).
PRICE: $40-50

Illustration 303.

128

Illustration 304.

Illustration 305.

Baby Coos (Coos family): HP head; magic skin body filled with foam; composition arms and bent legs; came in 14in (35.6cm), 16in (40.6cm), 18in (45.7cm), 20in (50.8cm), 22in (55.9cm); sleep eyes; closed mouth.

A description in the company catalog stated, "She cries if you squeeze her hard, sobs if you spank her, coos when you squeeze her gently. She can be washed, bathed, and powdered like a real baby." She came with an organdy dress and bonnet, slip, socks, and shoes plus a tiny tea set.

A more expensive baby came with a deluxe head. She could also be purchased in a larger size (life size). Still another deluxe model came with a wardrobe of organdy dresses, bonnet, slip, bed jacket, socks, feeding plate and spoon, three powder puffs and the set was packed in airplane luggage.

MARKS: "Ideal Doll, Made in U.S.A." or "16 Ideal Doll, Made in U.S.A."

SEE: *Illustration 304* (head). *(Ruth Glover Collection.) Illustration 305* (doll) (page TD5, Ideal's Doll Catalog, 1951).

PRICE: $40-50

Illustration 307.

Illustration 306.

Brother Coos (Coos family):   This was the same doll as *Baby Coos* but dressed in long overalls, basque shirt and a cap. He also came in the 27in (68.6cm) size in the deluxe model. He was packed in a deluxe acetate window gift box.

   MARKS: "Ideal Doll, Made in U.S.A." or "16 Ideal Doll, Made in U.S.A."
   SEE: *Illustration 306* (page TD6, Ideal's Doll Catalog, 1951).
   PRICE: $40-50

Sister Coos (Coos family):   This doll is part of a matching set to *Brother Coos*. She is dressed in a short skirt, basque shirt and beret. It came in a deluxe acetate window gift box.

   MARKS: "Ideal Doll, Made in U.S.A." or "16 Ideal Doll, Made in U.S.A."
   SEE: *Illustration 307* (page TD5, Ideal's Doll Catalog, 1951).
   PRICE: $40-50

Illustration 308.

"Original Ideal Catalog not available for better photograph."

Illustration 309.

Illustration 310.

Howdy Doody: *Howdy Doody* was one of the very first hard plastic dolls in 1947. He had a movable jaw which could be manipulated like a ventriloquist's dummy by pulling a string in back of the head. He was authentically dressed like the TV puppet with a plaid shirt and twill dungarees and boots with a scarf around his neck. His body was stuffed. 20½in (52.1cm) and 25in (64.8cm); 1947-1955.

MARKS: "Ideal" (head)

SEE: *Illustration 308* (page A-10, Ideal's Doll Catalog, 1952).

PRICE: Not enough price samples available.

Baby Plassie (Plassie family).   HP head/arms/legs; sizes from 16in (40.6cm) to 24in (61cm); sleep eyes with lashes; crying voice that sounded like real baby; open mouth with teeth; mohair wig or molded hair; also had vinyl arms and legs; organdy dress and bonnet; she was priced according to the clothes on each doll.

MARKS: "P. 50 Ideal, Made in U.S.A." (head); or "Ideal Doll, Made in U.S.A. #2252077."

SEE: *Illustration 309* (page 12, Ideal's Doll Catalog, 1949-50).

PRICE: $40-50

Plassie Toddler (Plassie family):   HP; sleep eyes; fully-jointed; open mouth with two teeth; mohair wig; felt tongue; composition arms and legs; cloth body; organdy party dress, embroidery, satin ribbon, slip, panties, bonnet, shoes and socks.

MARKS: "P-50 Made in U.S.A." (head)

SEE: *Illustration 310* (page 15, Ideal's Doll Catalog 1949-50).

PRICE: $40-50

Illustration 311.

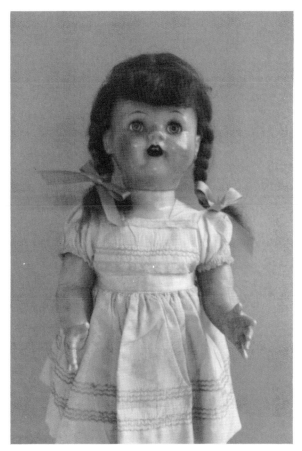

Illustration 312.

Saucy Walker (Saucy Walker family):   This doll came in a girl and boy version; circa 1952. This large 22in (55.9cm) doll was the first big doll to walk according to the Ideal Company catalog. *Saucy* is an excellent quality doll with a beautiful expression on her face. There were many imitations of *Saucy* on the market with varying degrees of quality. Ideal did make dolls for other companies and distributors, and there are pictures of some *Saucy Walker* types with no marks and Ideal characteristics at the end of the Ideal section.

HP: 22in (55.9cm); jointed head turning walker; flirty rolling eyes; saran wig which could be brushed and waved; grill in stomach (see Identification Guide, page 276D); open mouth with two teeth; individual fingers; painted eyelashes under eyes; pinjointed walker with unpainted Ideal screw type pin (see Identification Guide, page 290B); straight legs; red dot in corner of eye; double crease behind knee; circa 1952.

MARKS: "Ideal" (head)

SEE: *Illustration 311* (green dress). *Illustration 312* (pink dress). *(Helen Krielow Collection).*

PRICE: $85-95

134

Illustration 313.

Saucy Walker Toddler (Saucy Walker family):   HP; 14in (35.6cm) and 16in (40.6cm); features similar to larger *Saucy Walker*; fully-jointed walker with straight legs; sleep eyes with lashes; lashes painted under eyes; open mouth with two teeth; HP tongue; feathered eyebrows; pin joint walker with unpainted screw type pin (see Identification Guide, page 290B); arms only lift to shoulder height; original clothes; red dots in inner corners of eyes; diamond seat, two dimples in front and two dimples on back of knee.

MARKS: "Ideal Doll W16" (head)

SEE: *Illustration 313* (page 1, Ideal's Doll Catalog, 1952). *Illustration 314.* Comparison of all HP doll (right) with the vinyl head doll (left).

PRICE: $60-80

Illustration 314.

Ideal's outstanding QUALITY and CRAFTSMANSHIP is pre-sold to America's Millions — with large scale national advertising and promotion. Ideal's Quality Dolls last longer, provide longer play. Your reputation, sales, profits — are built on QUALITY merchandise! That's why it pays you to push *Ideal's Walking Dolls!*

IDEAL'S FAMOUS ORIGINAL WALKING DOLL

SAUCY WALKER

She walks, flirts, sits, cries. She turns her head from side to side and rolls her eyes. Vinyl head with rooted Saran wig. Fully jointed with concealed walking mechanism. No key to wind, nothing to go out of order. Her exquisite long Saran hair can be combed, brushed and waved. She has plastic curlers. High styled outfits include slip, panties, socks and vinyl shoes. Packed: Each in box.

No.	Size	Packed	Weight
2009	17"	1 doz.	33 lbs.
2019	23"	½ doz.	30 lbs.
2012	17" Hat & Coat	1 doz.	33 lbs.
2013	23" Hat & Coat	½ doz.	30 lbs.

Illustration 315

Saucy Walker *(Saucy Walker* family): vinyl head; HP; 23in (58.4cm); head turning walker; arms only lift to shoulder heights; flirty, rolling sleep eyes with lashes; delicate lashes painted under eyes; dimple in knees; individual fingers; diamond seat; double crease behind knees; straight legs; regular walking mechanism (not pin jointed); grill in stomach (see Identification Guide, page 276E); she is larger than the HP *Saucy.*

MARKS: "Ideal Doll VP 23" (head)

SEE: *Illustration 315* (Ideal's Doll Catalog, 1955). *Illustration 316* (doll). *Illustration 317* (close-up).

Illustration 316.

Illustration 317.

Illustration 318.

Saucy Walker Toddler *(Saucy Walker* family): vinyl head; HP body; 17in (43.2cm); head turning walker with screw type pin walker (see Identification Guide, page 290B); straight legs; individual fingers; grill in stomach (see Identification Guide, page 277I); sleep eyes with lashes; delicate painted lashes under eyes; dimples on knees both front and back; diamond seat; white print dress under maroon zipper jacket; gray collar and sleeves; 1955.

MARKS: "VP" (head); "Ideal Doll W 16" (body)

SEE: *Illustration 314* (comparison picture on page 135). *Illustration 318.*

Comparison picture of the doll made from HP (right) and the doll with the vinyl head (left) sharing a trunk full of clothes.

PRICE: $40-60

Illustration 319.

Posie, the Walking Doll of a Hundred Life-Like Poses *(Saucy Walker* family): vinyl head; HP body; 23in (58.4cm); magic knee joint so *Posie* can kneel to pray; she sits in a chair, walks, bends her knees; saran rooted hair that can be shampooed and styled; sleep eyes; individual fingers; closed mouth; fully jointed with knee joints; normal walking mechanism (not pin jointed); diamond seat; grill in stomach (see Identification Guide, page 277H).

    MARKS: "Ideal Doll" (head); "Ideal Doll" (body); "Pat. Pending" (back of upper leg)

    SEE: *Illustration 319* (Ideal's Doll Catalog, 1955). *Illustration 320* (white dress with red and blue print). (Pat Parton Collection.) *Illustration 321* (markings). *(Pat Parton Collection.)*

    PRICE: $50-70

Illustration 320.

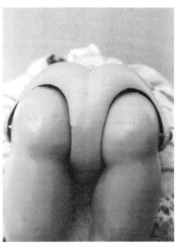

Illustration 321.

Illustration 322.

Illustration 323.

***Posie* Toddler** *(Saucy Walker* family): vinyl head; HP body; 17in (43.2cm); head turning walker with screw pin joint (see Identification Guide, page 290B); individual fingers; fully-jointed including knees; dimples on front of knees; grill in stomach (see Identification Guide, page 277I); sleep eyes with lashes; closed mouth; yellow cotton dress with white lace collar; delicate eyelashes under eyes; feathered eyebrows; 1955.
MARKS: "Ideal Doll VP 17" (head); "Ideal Doll W 16" (body)
SEE: *Illustration 322.*
PRICE: $40-50

Tiny Girl: HP; 9in (22.9cm); walker with turning head; pin jointed walker; pin covered with paint; two dimples on knee; painted-molded hair with curls covering ear; individual fingers; closed mouth; molded lashes; not original clothes; circa 1950.
MARKS: "Ideal Doll 9" (body and head)
SEE: *Illustration 323.*
PRICE: $15-20

Illustration 324.

Toni Family:

Common Characteristics: HP; closed mouth; sleep eyes with lashes; painted lashes below eyes; individual fingers with four dimples on back of hand; two dimples behind the knee; standard arm (see Identification Guide, page 262A); line around wrist; usually well marked; pretty flesh tone; $\curlyvee$ on seat; washable, curlable hair.

    MARKS: "Ideal Doll"
       "P 90" 14in (35.6cm)
       "P 91" 16in (40.6cm)
       "P 92" 19in (48.3cm)
       "P 93" 21in (53.3cm)
       "P 94" 22½in (57.2cm)

Toni dolls: According to the Ideal 75th Anniversary booklet, "Perhaps the biggest sensation of the period was the Toni doll, a fashion doll which became the first doll in history to wear a nylon wig that could be shampooed and permanented by embryonic beauticians. But the real success of the Toni doll was attributable not just to its life-like hair, but to Ben Michton's special talents for promotion. He enlisted the help of 12 Paris couturiers to design trend-setting fashions for the doll, thereby creating not only a product within a product, but a rage within the industry. The ads of that period introducing the doll said it all: 'Not since Madame Pompadour decreed tresses has there been such a furor in fashion. Twelve Toni dolls went to Paris...and had dresses designed just for them by the world's leading designers'."

    The dolls advertised Toni home permanents and curlers which came with the doll. An advertisement said, "There's enough nylon in Toni's wig to make 7 pairs of 15 denier nylon hose selling at $2.00 a pair." They also came with a Toni Play Wave.

    SEE: *Illustration 324 (Private Collection.)*

Illustration 325.

Illustration 326.

***Toni* dolls;** see characteristics previously listed.

MARKS: See *Toni* doll's common characteristics.

SEE: *Illustration 325.* From left to right; all original clothes; P 90; red skirt and blouse; *(Thelma Purvis Collection).* P 92 (walker); pink organdy dress, blue ribbon, white collar. P 93; pink cotton dress with blue trim. P 91; green and yellow print dress. *Illustration 326.* Doll in red, white and blue original clothes. *(Private Collection.) Illustration 327* (page D5, Ideal's Doll Catalog 1952).

PRICE: P90 $80-95

P91 $100-110

P92 $115-125

P93 $125-150

P94 Not enough samples available

Illustration 327.

Toni Walker (*Toni* family): HP; see *Toni* common characteristics; feathered eyebrows; eye shadow on upper eyes; hip pin walker with Ideal; unpainted pin joint (see Identification Guide, page 290B); circa 1953.

    MARKS: See common marks of *Toni* dolls; a few walkers have a "W" after the *Toni* number.

    SEE: *Illustration 328* (W mark).

    PRICE: $80-95

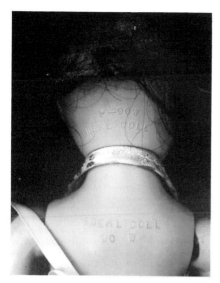

Illustration 328.

Illustration 330.

Illustration 329.

Walking Girl: vinyl head/arms; HP body; 25in (63.5cm); rooted hair; sleep eyes; jointed at neck, arms, legs, elbows, knees; hair can be shampooed.

    MARKS: Unknown

    SEE: *Illustration 329* (Ideal's Doll Catalog, 1955). *Illustration 330* (Ideal's Doll Catalog, 1955).

    PRICE: $50-55

148

Illustration 331.

Illustration 332.

***Harriet Hubbard Ayer** (Toni* family):   vinyl head; HP body; came in 14in (35.6cm), 16in (40.6cm), 19in (48.3cm), and 21in (53.3cm); *Harriet Hubbard Ayer* created a line of famous cosmetics. This lovely doll was named after her, and a beauty kit came with the doll; her vinyl face was very pale so that the little mother could practice applying makeup; beauty kit was mounted on the doll's own lovely beauty table; an illustrated book of instructions came with the doll; she had common characteristics of the *Toni* family; gray dress with attached pants; green and white pinafore. Pinafore also came in red and blue stripes.

   MARKS: "MK 14 Ideal Doll" (head); "Ideal Doll P 90" (back)
   SEE: *Illustration 331* (doll). *Illustration 332* (close-up). *Illustration 333* (page 1, Ideal's Doll Catalog, 1953).
   PRICE: $95-125

Illustration 334.

Illustration 335.

Miss Curity -- The First Lady of First Aid *(Toni* family):   HP; see characteristics of *Toni* family; 14in (35.6cm); eye shadow.

According to an Ideal advertisement, *Miss Curity* was the most famous nurse in America. She was nationally advertised by Bauer and Black in the country's leading publications and featured in full color displays in 15,000 drug stores coast to coast and on network TV and radio. She came complete with a Curity First Aid Kit and a booklet of first-aid play instructions. She is dressed in an authentic nurse's outfit of starched white with white socks, shoes, nurse's cap and red and blue cape. She has washable curlable hair.

The play nurse kit consists of adhesive tape, Curad plastic bandages, wrist watch, hypo needle, sugar pills, sterile pads, Curity absorbent cotton, fever thermometer, tongue depressor, scissors, progress chart and special nurse's instructions.

MARKS: "P 90, Ideal Doll Made in USA" (head); "Ideal Doll P 90" (back)
SEE: *Illustration 334. Illustration 335* (page D3, Ideal's Doll Catalog, 1953).
PRICE: $90-100

Illustration 336.

Miss Curity: HP; 7½in (19.1cm); dressed in white oilcloth type dress; nurse's hat which says, "Miss Curity;" sleep eyes; painted eyelashes above eyes; heart-shaped mouth; Virga-type shoes (see Identification Guide, page 284F); white nurse uniform; painted white stockings and shoes; 2nd and 3rd fingers molded together; mold flaw below wrist; net underpants; 1953. This doll was mentioned in Ideal's Doll Catalog with a list number of "2810."

MARKS: None
SEE: *Illustration 336.*
PRICE: $15-20

Illustration 337.

Illustration 338.

Mary Hartline *(Toni* family): "Television's Beautiful Circus Princess;" HP; long blonde hair, *Mary Hartline*'s trademark; (see *Toni* family characteristics); she wears an authentic copy of Mary's drum majorette TV costume including the familiar white boots and baton; heavy eye shadow; child sized baton -- not doll size; she came with red, green and blue dresses.

    MARKS: "Ideal Doll Made in U.S.A." (head); "Ideal Doll P-91" (body)

    SEE: *Illustration 337* (doll). *Illustration 338* (page D7, Ideal's Doll Catalog, 1952). Catalog, 1952).

    PRICE: $100-130

Illustration 339.

Mary Hartline: HP; 7½in (19.1cm); shiny plastic; Virga-type painted, molded boots; eyelashes above eyes; 2nd and 3rd fingers molded together; red dress with white trim. This doll is mentioned in Ideal's Doll Catalog with a list number of "1250."
MARKS: "Ideal Doll" (back)
SEE: *Illustration 339* (page D7, Ideal's Doll Catalog, 1952).
PRICE: $20-30

Illustration 340.

Betsy McCall *(Toni* family):   vinyl head; HP body; 14in (35.6cm); closed mouth; sleep eyes and lashes; she wears real Betsy McCall clothes just like the dresses little girls shop for at department stores; fully-jointed; an easy-to-sew pattern came with every *Betsy McCall;* there were also paper dolls of Betsy each month in *McCall's Magazine,* 1953.

   MARKS: "McCall Corp." (head); "P 90, Ideal Doll" (back)

   SEE: *Illustration 340* (doll; white blouse, black, purple and blue skirt). *Illustration 341* (page D3, Ideal's Doll Catalog, 1952). *Illustration 342* (page D4, Ideal's Doll Catalog, 1953).

   PRICE: $100-130

Illustration 341.

Illustration 342.

"Original Ideal Catalog not available for better photograph."

156

Illustration 343.

"Original Ideal Catalog not available for better photograph."

Illustration 344.

Sara Ann *(Toni* family):   she came with the regular *Toni* features and sizes. It is difficult to identify her unless she comes in the original box; 1952.
    MARKS: "Made in USA" (head); "Ideal Doll P 90" (body)
    SEE: *Illustration 343* (D5 Ideal's Doll Catalog, 1953).
    PRICE: $95-105

Princess Mary *(Toni* family):   vinyl head; HP; 16in (40.6cm), 19in (48.3cm), 21in (53.3cm); head turning walker; fully-jointed; rooted hair; came with plastic curlers; closed mouth; feathered eyebrows; pin jointed walker with screw (see Identification Guide, page 290B); standard walker arm (see Identification Guide, page 263E); the *Princess Mary* bride came in just the 14in (35.6cm) and 19in (48.3cm).
    MARKS: "V92" (head); "V19" (back)
    SEE: *Illustration 344* (twins; pink dress with blue trim). *(Pat Parton Collection.)*
    Illustration 345 (Ideal's Doll Catalog, 1955).
    PRICE: $50-75

Illustration 345.

Illustration 346.

EASIER TO COMB!
WILL NOT SNARL!

HAIR WILL NOT COMB OUT!

STRONG! DURABLE!

Ruth

IDEAL'S GIRL DOLL
WITH MAGIC ROOTED HAIR

Illustration 347.

Ruth *(Toni* family): vinyl head; HP body; came in sizes 17in (43.2cm), 19in (48.3cm), 21in (53.3cm); the advertisement said, "All plastic, fully jointed girl doll. She has lustrous saran wig inserted strand by strand in doll's vinyl head. She came with curlers. She has sleep eyes and lashes;" she had a deluxe taffeta party dress with nylon net slip and cotton panties.

MARKS: Unknown
SEE: *Illustration 346* (doll). *(Pat Parton Collection.) Illustration 347* (page D9, Ideal's Doll Catalog, 1952).
PRICE: $50-75

Illustration 348.

"Original Ideal Catalog not available for better photograph."

Illustration 349.

Ideal did make unnamed, unpromoted dolls for the mass market. The 1949-50 Ideal catalog had their pictures as shown in *Illustration 348* and *349*.

Unnamed Girl: HP; fully-jointed; sleep eyes with lashes; mohair wig; closed mouth; individual fingers.
 1. Girl in long party gown, 19in (48.3cm).
  SEE: *Illustration 348* (page 15, Ideal's Doll Catalog, 1949-50).
  PRICE: $50-60

Girl: HP; fully-jointed; lucite sleep eyes and lashes; ankle length dresses; closed mouth; 19in (48.3cm) and 21in (53.3cm).
  SEE: *Illustration 349* (Ideal's Doll Catalog 1949-50).
  PRICE: $50-60

Illustration 350.

Unknown doll with Ideal characteristics: girl: HP; 17in (43.3cm); pin jointed head turning walker, screw pin joint (see Identification Guide, page 290B); open mouth; two teeth; individual fingers; red print dress with white collar and sleeves.

  MARKS: "Ideal" (head); "Eegee" (body). This is a classic example of a "mixed-up" doll. The owner has consulted experts, and they all say that there has been no marriage (repair with parts from other dolls). She is mint and in unplayed with condition.

  SEE: *Illustration 350. (Sandy Strater Collection.)*
  PRICE: $60-75

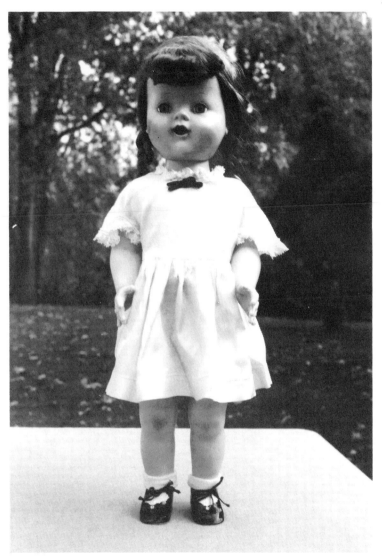

Unknown dolls with Ideal characteristics: girl; HP; 22in (55.9cm); yellow dress; open/closed mouth with molded tongue; inexpensive quality of HP; lovely flesh color; sleep eyes with lashes, pin jointed head turning walker with screws used as pins (see Identification Guide, page 290B).

MARKS: △ (neck)

SEE: *Illustration 351. (Pat Parton Collection.)*

PRICE: $40-50

162

Illustration 352.

Unknown dolls with Ideal characteristics: girl; HP; wearing party dress.
MARKS: None
SEE: *Illustration 352. (Pat Parton Collection.)*
PRICE: $35-45

Illustration 353.

Unknown doll with Ideal characteristics: bride; HP; 22in (55.9cm); open mouth; two teeth; felt tongue; sleep eyes and lashes; dark lashes beneath eyes; individual fingers with dimples under fingers; pin jointed walker with Ideal screw type pins; head turning walker; diamond seat; two dimple-like depressions on back; not original clothes; grill (see Identification Guide, page 276F).

MARKS: △ (neck); 8 (upper back)

SEE: *Illustration 353* (close-up).

PRICE: $40-50

IMPERIAL CROWN TOY CO.
(Imperial * Impco)

It is difficult to find many references to Imperial Crown Toy Company in the published doll research. However, many collectors have enjoyed these dolls for years, and they are not difficult to find. Most of the hard plastic dolls from this company date to the very early 1950s, and they were among the early experimenters in the change to the new vinyl head with the rooted hair. A few of their dolls are rather sticky today, but others are in excellent condition, with beautiful serious faces and excellent flesh color.

It is interesting to note that the company experimented with unusual wigs as well as rooted hair. Many of their baby and child dolls had lambswool or caracul wigs. Some of the girl dolls had fine examples of human hair or early synthetic wigs.

Many of the dolls are unmarked but can be easily identified through the characteristics of the pictured dolls.

Girl: vinyl head; HP; 16in (40.6cm); beautiful, curly light brown washable wig; closed mouth; excellent flesh tone to the vinyl; sleep eyes with lashes; jointed at neck, arms, legs; non-walker; individual fingers; dimples on back of knees; °Y° on seat, (see Identification Guide, page 282B); wrist line all around wrist; dimples below fingers on hand; standard arm hook; pronounced breasts; unusually large stomach; navel with circle in center; heavy shoulder muscles; not original clothes; circa 1950. not original clothes; circa 1950.
    MARKS: "IMPCO" (head)
    SEE: *Illustration 354. Illustration 355* (side view of stomach).
    PRICE: $35-45

Blonde Impco: vinyl head; HP; same description as doll in *Illustration 355;* clothes not original; eye shadow; circa 1950.
    MARKS: "Imperial" (head)
    SEE: *Illustration 356. (Barbara Comienski Collection.)*
    PRICE: $35-45

Illustration 354.   *Illustration 355.*   *Illustration 356.*

Illustration 357.

Illustration 358.

Illustration 359.

Walking Doll: HP; 18in (45.7cm); open mouth with five teeth and felt tongue; red hair; diamond seat (see Identification Guide, page 282A); individual widespread fingers; pin hip walker with screw-type pin (see Identification Guide, page 290B); standard walker arm joint; cryer grill (see Identification Guide, page 277J); not original clothes; head turns; circa 1950.

> **MARKS:** "Impco" (head)
> **SEE:** *Illustration 357.*
> **PRICE:** $25-30

Girl: HP; 17in (43.2cm); open mouth with four teeth; °Y° on seat; unusual fur wig; sleep eyes with lashes; black eye shadow; unusual ears with molded hair over them; same body characteristics as other Imperial girl; very wide individual fingers; red flowered dress with white yoke; circa 1951.

> **MARKS:** "Imperial Crown Doll Co. Made in USA;" or none
> **SEE:** *Illustration 358.*
> **PRICE:** $35-45

Girl: HP; 19½in (49.6cm); open mouth with four teeth; sleep eyes with lashes; mohair wig; dark painted lashes under eyes; unpainted hip rivet (see Identification Guide, page 290C); head turning walker; navel has circle in center; individual fingers; blue plaid dress; circa 1951.

> **MARKS:** "IMPCO"
> **SEE:** *Illustration 359. (Pat Parton Collection.)*
> **PRICE:** $25-35

166

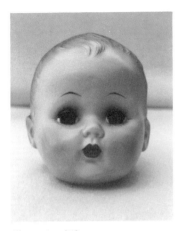

Illustration 360.

Illustration 361.

Baby: HP head; open mouth nurser with rubber tube for liquid; small rubber tongue; molded hair; sleep eyes and lashes; pretty doll with good quality plastic; black eye shadow; circa 1951.
MARKS: "Imperial Crown Toy, Made in U.S.A."
SEE: *Illustration 360* (head).
(Ruth Glover Collection.)
PRICE: $30-35 (entire doll)

Girl: HP; 10½in (26.7cm); chubby type; closed mouth; sleep eyes; red dress; striped bodice; circa 1950.
MARKS: "Impco" (head)
SEE: *Illustration 361. (Rosemary Romance Collection.)*
PRICE: $20-30

DOLLS NOT PHOTOGRAPHED
Imperial made several babies with caracul wigs. They had HP heads and were marked: "Imperial" or "Imperial Crown Toy Co., Made in U.S.A."

INDIANS

Many people bought Indian souvenir dolls when traveling, at sportsman shows or at other events. Frequently these Indian dolls were purchased undressed from doll manufacturers such as Plastic Molded Arts and dressed by Indians, craftsmen and small companies. The quality and authenticity vary greatly.

Other Indian dolls were completely manufactured, dressed and sold by doll companies. Again, quality varied.

Illustration 362.

Illustration 363.

Illustration 364.

Illustration 365.

Indian Boy and Girl:

Indian Girl: HP; 6in (15.2cm); sleep eyes; mohair wig; gauntlet hands, molded Knickerbocker-type hair under a wig; mold mark under wrist like Beehler Art; shoes (see Identification Guide, page 264L).

    MARKS: None (girl)

    SEE: *Illustration 362. (Pat Parton Collection.)*

Indian Boy: HP; painted side glancing eyes; molded hair; shoes (see Identification Guide, page 264I); gauntlet hands; rattles when played with.

    MARKS: "Knickerbocker Plastic Co. Glendale, California, Des. Pat. Pending."

    SEE: *Illustration 362. (Pat Parton Collection.)*

    PRICE: $5-15 each

Two Girls: HP; doll on right - 7½in (19.1cm); Virga characteristics; mitten hands; side glancing eyes; Virga type shoes (see Identification Guide, page 264E); jointed only at arms; one-piece body; leather costumes.

    MARKS: None

Doll on left - painted side glancing eyes; one line on seat; Virga characteristics.

    MARKS: None

Both dolls made by the same company but they are very different.

    SEE: *Illustration 363. (Pat Parton Collection.)*

    PRICE: $5-15 each

Girl: HP; 7½in (19.1cm); fluttery sleep eyes; one line on seat; Virga-Fortune characteristics; shoes (see Identification Guide, page 284E); blue leather dress.

MARKS: None

SEE: *Illustration 364. (Pat Parton Collection.)*

PRICE: $5-15

Duchess Indian Girl: HP; 7½in (19.1cm); sleep eyes; painted eyelashes above eyes; Duchess characteristics and arm hook (see Identification Guide, page 268V).

MARKS: "Duchess Doll Corp, Design Copyright, 1948"

SEE: *Illustration 365. (Pat Parton Collection.)*

PRICE: $5-15

Illustration 366.

Three Indian Girls:

Left: Mother and Papoose: HP; 7½in (19.1cm) sleep eyes with painted lashes; PMA characteristics (see Plastic Molded Arts); nicely beaded leather dress and shoes; papoose has side glancing eyes; jointed arms and legs; painted hair.

MARKS: None

Middle: HP; 7½in (19.1cm); PMA characteristics; leather suit painted and beaded.

MARKS: None

Right: HP; 7½in (19.1cm); Virga-Fortune characteristics (see page 240); gauntlet hands; one-piece body with only jointed arms; painted and beaded dress.

MARKS: None

SEE: *Illustration 366. (Pat Parton Collection.)*

PRICE: $5-15 each

IRWIN

The Irwin Company was one of the earliest companies that changed into the production of hard plastic dolls. Their most famous dolls were babies that were widely used by crochet enthusiasts. However, they also made a 15in (38.1cm) baby in 1948 which could drink and wet. By that time they were also making character dolls in a wide variety of shapes and sizes.

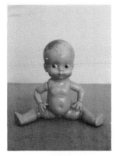

Illustration 367.   *Illustration 368.*

Baby: HP; 5in (12.7cm) and 8½in (21.6cm); jointed at legs and shoulder; black painted side glancing eyes; brown hair; very shiny hard plastic; late 1940s.
MARKS: "Irwin"(in circle) with banner running through it.
SEE: *Illustration 367. (Phyllis Appell Collection.)*
PRICE: $8-15

Bashful Boy or Girl: HP; 6in (15.2cm); jointed at shoulders only; painted side glancing eyes; closed mouth; open hands with palm down; often seen with crocheted clothes; very shiny plastic; late 1940s.
MARKS: "Irwin" (in circle) with banner running through it
SEE: *Illustration 368.*
PRICE: $8-15

KNICKERBOCKER

Girl: HP; 6in (15.2cm); vinyl arms; gauntlet hands; side glancing eyes; painted and molded curly hair with raised loop for bow; white and navy polka dot dress; jointed only at arms, shoes (see Identification Guide, page 286L).
MARKS: "Knickerbocker" (body)
SEE: *Illustration 369. (Pat Parton Collection.)*
PRICE: $5-10

Illustration 369.   *Illustration 370.*

Indians: HP; 6in (15.2cm); same characteristics as girl; purchased at Cleveland, Ohio, Sportsman Show, 1965.
MARKS: "Knickerbocker" (body)
SEE: *Illustration 370. (Dolly Jakubecz Collection.)*
PRICE: $5-10 each

LATEXTURE PRODUCTS

This mannequin was advertised as the first plastic doll. It was made all in one piece plastic which looks like wood or papier-mâché. It was made during World War II for little girls, so they could help the war effort by learning how to sew. The patterns in the box were labeled Maison Blanche Co. #12M 39873. They cost 19¢

Illustration 371.

Fashion Doll: (Marianne Fashion); advertised as a mannequin, not an ordinary doll; miniature of a teenage girl; arms detach to make fitting easier; pegs on feet to fit into stand; patterns available for 12½in (31.8cm) and 15in (39.4cm) model. She wears the ubiquitious black dress of the period with a pearl necklace; circa 1943 to 1945.
    MARKS: "Latexture © NYC" (middle of back)
    SEE: *Illustration 371.*
    PRICE: $50

H. D. LEE

Buddy Lee was the trademark doll of H. D. Lee Co. The dolls were dressed as train engineers, cowboys, industrial doll and others.

Buddy Lee: HP; 13in (33cm); molded painted hair; painted side glancing eyes; four fingers molded together; heavily painted eyelashes on upper eyes and bold heavy brown eyebrows; painted on black high shoes; molded on ears placed on separately; closed smile; long metal wire pieces at armholes; stands alone nicely; blue coveralls; circa 1949.
    MARKS: Buddy Lee (in large letters)
    SEE: *Illustration 372. (Private Collection.)*
    PRICE: $140-170

Illustration 372.

LENCI

A most unusual doll is pictured here. The name, Lenci, brings visions of beautifully dressed felt dolls. However, this hard plastic 12in (30.5cm) doll is in a very different mode. She does have a "look" about her that sets her apart from all other hard plastic dolls. She is dressed in a fashionable pink silk dress.

After World War II, Lenci dolls in hard plastic were produced, but very little is known about them. Often labels were sewn into the clothes on the inside.

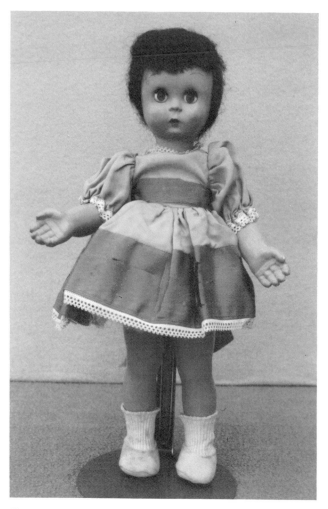

Illustration 373.

Illustration 374.

Illustration 375.

Illustration 376.

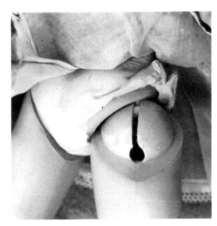

Illustration 377.

Girl: HP; 12in (30.5cm); large, dark sleep eyes with lashes; very large hands with 1st, 2nd, 3rd, 4th fingers molded together; painted mouth; black mohair wig with felt flowers; pink silk dress with white trim; label on dress.

MARKS: None on body; (label) "Lenci Torino"

SEE: *Illustration 373* (doll). *(Heloise Miles Collection.) Illustration 374* (face). *(Heloise Miles Collection.) Illustration 375* (inside of dress). *(Heloise Miles Collection.) Illustration 376* (flowers in hair). *(Heloise Miles Collection.) Illustration 377* (strung legs). *(Heloise Miles Collection.)*

PRICE: No price given on this doll because of its rarity and lack of price samples.

LITTLE NURSE DOLL CO.
(Cedar Rapids, Iowa)

One of the joys of doll research is the unexpected stories of even the small dolls. This doll is one of the nicer inexpensive hard plastic dolls. Her nurse's dress was made with loving care. While a few seams were sewn on the machine, most of the work was done carefully by hand. The tiny seal in blue and white was carefully designed to compliment the blue and white nurse's uniform.

Nurse: HP; 7½in (19.1cm); one-piece body with arm and neck joints; Fortune-Virga characteristics; painted molded shoes (see Identification Guide, page 284E); painted white nurse's stockings; individually molded fingers; inset sleep eyes; painted eyelashes above eyes; high arched eyebrows; standard armhook; red wig; white uniform; blue blouse.

MARKS: "11" (left arm); "8" (right arm); seal on dress "Little Nurse Doll Co.//224 18th St. S.E. Cedar Rapids, Iowa."

SEE: *Illustration 378.*

PRICE: $10-15

Illustration 378.

LOVELY DOLL

Illustration 379.

Illustration 380.

In 1956 or 1957 Polly Judd dressed 100 small fashion dolls for a charity bazaar. She bought a gross of undressed dolls from a toy wholesaler on Detroit Avenue in Cleveland, Ohio. Pam was a small girl, and she loved them all. She was allowed to keep a few for her Christmas tree.

The two Santa's helpers survived through the years, and they still grace her tree. The molded shoes and fluttery eyes give clues to their origin.

Snow White: HP; 7in (17.8cm); fluttery sleep eyes; glued on wig; one-piece body; arm and neck joints; painted on eyelashes above eyes; high arched eyebrows; 2nd and 3rd fingers molded together; painted on shoes with bows (see Identification Guide, page 286J); standard arm hook; two marks on palms of hands; two lines under nose; black wig; white dress with black glitter; circa 1954.

> **MARKS:** None; box marked "A Lovely Doll, Movable Eyes, Movable Arms, Movable head."
> **SEE:** *Illustration 379.*
> **PRICE:** $10-15

Santa's Helper with One Package: HP; 7in (17.8cm); same characteristics as *Snow White*; green felt dress and hat; red Christmas trim.

> **MARKS:** None
> **SEE:** *Illustration 380.*
> **PRICE:** $10-15

Illustration 381.   *Illustration 382.*   *Illustration 383.*

Santa's Helper with two packages: HP; 7in (17.8cm); same characteristics as *Snow White;* white dress; red and green glitter.
  MARKS: None
  SEE: *Illustration 381.*
  PRICE: $10-15

Another doll dressed by hand is this Amish Girl: HP; 7in (17.8cm); same characteristics as *Snow White;* maroon cotton dress and cape; white cap.
  MARKS: None
  SEE: *Illustration 382.*
  PRICE: $10-15

UNKNOWN DOLL WITH LOVELY CHARACTERISTICS:
Tastee Freeze Sweetheart (see Duchess):   HP; 7in (17.8cm); fluttery sleep eyes; glued on wig; one-piece body; arm and neck joints; painted on eyelashes above eyes; 2nd and 3rd fingers molded together; painted molded shoes with bows (see Identification Guide, page 286J); standard arm hook with extra ridge; two marks on palm of hands; two lines under nose; red lace bodice; white skirt with red hearts and flowers; red heart hat.
  MARKS: None
  SEE: *Illustration 383.*
  PRICE: $10-15

MADE IN U.S.A.

These dolls appear very often in collections, doll shows and in doll books. They vary greatly in the quality of the hard plastic and in the quality of the actual facial and body characteristics. Many, many of them are 14in (35.6cm). They have both closed and open mouths.

No book about hard plastic dolls would be complete without mention of these dolls. The Valentine *Lu Ann Simms* is one example. Desota has been known to use this marking. Roberta sometimes has the mark enclosed in a circle. Horsman also used it. American Character has used it for *Sweet Sue*.

Illustration 384.

Illustration 385.

Girl: shiny HP; 14in (35.6cm); sleep eyes; 2nd and 3rd fingers molded together; standard arm joint (see Identification Guide, page 262A); open mouth; four teeth; lace dress not original.

    MARKS: "Made in U.S.A." (back); "14" (head)
    SEE: *Illustration 384. (Phyllis Appell Collection.)*
    PRICE: $35-55

Girl: HP; 19in (48.3cm); sleep eyes with lashes; eyelashes painted below eyes; open mouth with six teeth; felt tongue; individual fingers; stockings with girdle and elastic garters; wrist line on palm side only; wide φ on seat; jointed at neck/arms/legs/ankles/knees; excellent quality HP with reddish flesh tone; not original clothes; circa 1951.

    MARKS: "Made in U.S.A." (faint; on waistline)
    SEE: *Illustration 385. (Barbara Comienski Collection.)*
    PRICE: $35-55

Illustration 387.

Illustration 386.

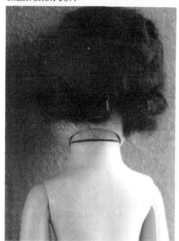

Illustration 388.

Blonde: HP; 14in (35.6cm); closed mouth; head turning walker; arm hook (see Identification Guide, page 262A); not original clothes.

    MARKS: "Made in U.S.A."

    SEE: *Illustration 386. (Barbara Comienski Collection.)*

    PRICE: $30-40

Brunette: HP; 14in (35.6cm); closed mouth; head turning walker; unpainted rivet hip joints (see Identification Guide, page 290C); two-piece neck; not original clothes.

    MARKS: "Made in U.S.A.;" "14" (head)

    SEE: *Illustration 387. (Laura Brown Collection.) Illustration 388* (mark). *(Laura Brown Collection.)*

    PRICE: $35-40

MAR

Walking doll: highly polished hard plastic; 9in (22.9cm); jointed at arms only; molded on blue clothes; key wind; when the doll walks the arms move up and down; individually molded fingers; circa 1951.

> **MARKS:** "Mars Made in USA" (in circle)
> **SEE:** *Illustration 389. (John Ezzo's childhood doll.)*
> **PRICE:** $15-25

Illustration 389.

MIDWESTERN MANUFACTURING CO.

(St. Louis, Missouri)

Girl: HP; 10½in (26.7cm); regular Plastic Molded Arts characteristics; dressed in Valentine dress; individually molded fingers; PMA shoes (see Identification Guide, page 283A); molded eyelashes; red bodice and ruffle; white skirt with red Valentines and flowers; blue felt hat; circa 1958.

> **MARKS:** None; "Midwestern Manufacturing Co." on box
> **SEE:** *Illustration 390.*
> **PRICE:** $15-30

Illustration 390.

MOLLYE

Mrs. Mollye Goldman was a part of the doll world for many years. She designed early Shirley Temple clothes and worked with Johnny Gruelle on the design of the *Raggedy Ann* and *Andy* dolls.

Her interest was wardrobe designing, and she worked for different companies. Among the companies were Horsman, Effanbee and Ideal.

She did market dolls under her own name and the doll costumes had excellent design and workmanship. Mollye's creations were in cloth, composition, hard plastic and later, vinyl.

Many of her dolls were not marked.

Illustration 391.

Illustration 392.

Ballerina-*Dancing Deb:* HP; vinyl head; open/closed mouth; sleep eyes; jointed shoulders, legs, knees, ankles for ballet slippers and high heels; unusually white body; painted lashes under eyes; 2nd and 3rd fingers molded together; legs have ridge at top (see Identification Guide, page 291); rather flat face; pink with silver net skirt and trim; silver metallic V inset bodice; circa 1954.

> **MARKS:** "x" (circle on head)
> **SEE:** *Illustration 391* (doll). *Illustration 392* (close-up).
> **PRICE:** $30-45

UNKNOWN DOLLS
WITH MOLLYE
CHARACTERISTICS:

Bride: Mollye loved to dress bride dolls, and she designed many beautiful wedding gowns for dolls. Often they were labeled. This doll is typical of the Horsman dolls that Mollye used, and the gown has the type of detail typical of Mollye. This is a magnificent doll; HP; 19in (48.3cm); platinum blonde curly hair; open mouth with four teeth; white lace and satin dress; white veil with jewels in crown; 1949 to 1953.

> **MARKS:** None; no label
> **SEE:** *Illustration 393. (Barbara Church Collection.)*
> **PRICE:** $100-125

Illustration 393.

Illustration 394.

Bride: This is another bride or bridesmaid dressed in lovely materials with the same attention to details. She is a brunette but is like some Horsman-type dolls with open mouth and four teeth; green nylon garden formal trimmed with white lace and pink and green flowers; matching hat; gold ribbon; carrying a flower bouquet; 1949 to 1953.
MARKS: None; no label
SEE: *Illustration 394. (Barbara Church Collection.)*
PRICE: $100-125

DOLLS NOT PHOTOGRAPHED:
Other all-HP dolls distributed by Mollye include an airline stewardess, business girl and various brides which seem to be unmarked.
Baby Joan and other babies had a HP head with cloth bodies and latex limbs. Some had a 450 mark.
A Betty Grable look-alike and other brides similar to the ballerina are marked with a circle x.
A Martha Washington-type doll was all HP with a one-piece body and legs with a white wig.
A 30in (76.2cm) *Lone Ranger* had a HP head and magic skin body.

MONICA

Hansi Share, originator, designer and manufacturer, experimented with rooted hair dolls in composition. Her dolls were beautiful and well made. About 1949 the company, Monica Studios, advertised a hard plastic doll. Her name was *Marion* and her hair was also rooted in hard plastic.

Illustration 395.

Marion (in box): HP; 18in (45.7cm); rooted hair; sleep eyes; pink dress with printed skirt and bolero.
MARKS: None on body
SEE: *Illustration 395. (Jane Gage Collection.)*
PRICE: $170-200

NANCY ANN

In the history of any form of art, an artist will stand out in an era. Such an artist was Nancy Ann Abbott. She designed clothes for a tiny, simply made pottery doll which captured the hearts of her generation and continued to be loved and collected until this present time. She named her doll simply *Nancy Ann*.

Because she had no experience in manufacturing, starting a doll company was not a simple matter for her but she persisted. To add to her problems, soon the United States was at war, and she, along with all of the people of the U.S.A., experienced the shortages and rationing of the time. Nancy Ann Abbott modified, used different types of clay, dipped the feet in paint, worried about cloth shortages and continued to delight the children of those dark years.

She met the challenge of using hard plastic with her customary inventiveness, and soon the small dolls were produced in this less breakable material for tiny fingers. The many dolls available to modern doll lovers today is a tribute to Nancy Ann's art and hard work.

Much has been written about the artist and her dolls. The books are all fascinating, and they explain in detail the changes which took place gradually.

MARKS: "Nancy Ann Story Book Dolls, USA Trademark, Reg." (the vast majority of these dolls were so marked)

IDENTIFICATION HINTS:

Collecting *Nancy Ann* dolls is a challenge for many doll lovers. Each new doll is exciting and identification is a beloved task. The following hints come from Marianne Gardner who has collected these Story Book dolls since childhood. She still follows up each lead to a new *Nancy Ann*, and her beautiful dolls are a joy to behold.

1. *Nancy Ann's* blue cloth usually fades to a light lavender or pinkish color.
2. Royal blue changes to purple.
3. The kelly green ribbon and cotton fades to gold.
4. All hard plastic type dolls have a woven florist type ribbon in varying widths. It is still sold today for 7-10¢ a yard in florist supply houses.
5. Most *Nancy Ann* hard plastic doll dresses have a brass snap closure on the back of the dress. A few of the late dresses were closed with a pin.
6. Brass snaps continued to be used until about 1956 when the metal was painted over with the color of the dress. By 1957, they had changed to a gripper snap which was continued until the company closed.
7. The marks are all the same, and they were continued when the dolls were manufactured in Hong Kong.

Nancy Ann was one of the first to go into the production of hard plastic dolls. By 1948, the first transitional hard plastic appeared. This continued to be the material generally used until the end of the company in the middle of the 1960s. With the exception of the first illustration, all dolls are hard plastic.

Illustration 396.

Illustration 397.

Starlight-Starbright: bisque with HP arms; transitional doll; dress was originally blue; 1948.

SEE: *Illustration 396. (Marianne Gardner Collection.)*
PRICE: $35-40

Pinch Face Dolls: transition from bisque to HP; 5½in (14cm); painted eyes; circa 1948 to 1950.

SEE: *Illustration 397. (Marianne Gardner Collection.)* From left to right (1) Yellow *Pretty as a Picture* with red hair. (2) Orchid *Bridesmaid* with blonde hair. (3) *Rain, Rain Go Away* dressed in yellow.
PRICE: $15-25

Illustration 400.

Illustration 398.

Illustration 399.   *Illustration 401.*

Painted Eye Dolls: circa 1951.
>   **SEE:** *Illustration 398. (Marianne Gardner Collection.)* From left to right: (1) *Little Miss Muffet;* yellow dress. (2) *Flowergirl;* white dress with blue trim. (3) *Topsey;* black doll; red plaid dress; red hair ribbon.
>   **PRICE:** $15-25 except for *Topsey* $25-40

Painted Eye Dolls: HP; 6-6½in (15.-16.5cm); used for months, operettas, hit parade; circa 1951.
>   **SEE:** *Illustration 399. (Marianne Gardner Collection.)* From left to right: (1) Blue; *June;* blue print taffeta dress; blue felt hat with white feather. (2) Yellow: *May*; yellow print taffeta dress; large yellow felt hat. (3) *Miss Independence: July;* red cape and hat; blue dress with red, white and blue trim.
>   **PRICE:** $20-35 (months); $30-45 (hit parade and operetta)

Dolls with black pupil sleep eyes: HP; 5½in (14cm); circa 1951 to 1952.
>   **SEE:** *Illustration 400. (Marianne Gardner Collection.)* From left to right: (1) *Lassie Fair;* pink dress with black lace trim. (2) *Sugar and Spice;* white and print dress with green trim. (3) *Alice Through the Looking Glass;* blue checked dress; white apron with red hearts. (4)*Alice Through the Looking Glass*; blue striped dress with apron.
>   **PRICE:** $15-30

Dolls with black pupil sleep eyes: HP, 6½in (16.5cm); 1951 to 1952.
>   **SEE:** *Illustration 401. (Marianne Gardner Collection.)* From right to left: (1) Yellow: *June;* yellow print taffeta dress, yellow hair ribbon. (2) Striped; *November*; pink and black striped taffeta dress; white lace trim; pink hair ribbon.
>   **PRICE:** $15-35

Illustration 402.

Illustration 403.

Illustration 404.

Dolls with black pupil sleep eyes: HP; 4½in (11.5cm); also came in 5½in (14cm) and 6½in (16.5cm); 1951 to 1952.

    SEE: *Illustration 402. (Marianne Gardner Collection.)* From left to right: (1) *Little Sister Goes to Sunday School;* there was a big sister with the same outfit; pink dress. (2) *Baby;* last one manufactured; white dress labeled: "Nancy Ann Christening." (3) *First Birthday.*

    PRICE: $20-35

Bride and Groom: HP; 6½in (16.5cm); unusual size for the bride doll; exquisite brocade gown; groom has painted eyes with flocked hair.

    SEE: *Illustration 403. (Marianne Gardner Collection.)*

    PRICE: $25-40

To Market: 5½in (14cm); waxy complexion; blue sleep eyes with lashes; dark pink bodice; light pink skirt decorated with strawberries; matching hat; 1954. This was the last Nancy Ann before the sale of the company. She was pictured in a store display poster and is a rare doll. The dress material was used for other dolls in the line. Nancy Ann *Style Show Doll* has on such a dress *(Illustration 409)*.

    SEE: *Illustration 404. (Marianne Gardner Collection.)*

    PRICE: $15-35

Illustration 405.

Illustration 406.

Hong Kong Doll: HP; doll in Nigeria outfit; made in Hong Kong; sold in plastic fronted boxes using the same trademark; white dress and veil; gold rickrack trim.

    SEE: *Illustration 405. (Marianne Gardner Collection.)*

    PRICE: $35

Brochure:

    SEE: *Illustration 406. (Marianne Gardner Collection.)*

Illustration 407.

Illustration 408.

Style Show Dolls: HP; 18-22in (45.7-55.9cm); saran hair wig; arched eyebrows; sleep eyes with lashes; closed mouth; slight bustline which often has two buttons on them; traces of the buttons make an excellent source of identification of these dolls; color on knees and wrists; smooth bisque-like flesh tone, wigs often were pulled back; slight black-gray eyeshadow; 2nd and 3rd fingers molded together and curved forward; excellent modeling of details on hands, wrists and ears; clothes were grown-up dresses. The dolls usually had long dresses which were made from beautiful laces and materials with lovely trim. The dresses often had hoops. The doll wore stockings and had satin shoes. The doll in *Illustration 408* is wearing a beige lace overskirt and bodice; turquoise ribbon and bow; turquoise sequins and trim at neck; circa 1950.

   MARKS: None on body; silver tag on wrist which listed the name of the doll and told of other available *Style Show Dolls.*

   SEE: *Illustration 407* (doll). *Illustration 408* (close-up).
   PRICE: $350-375

188

Illustration 409.

Illustration 411.

Illustration 410.

Style Show Doll: HP; 18in (45.7cm); wearing pink strawberry dress; see characteristics of other *Style Show Doll;* the dress material is unusual, but it was also used on the tiny Storybook Doll, see *Illustration 404*; it has also been seen in a long dress version and is pictured in the Style Show brochure. This doll was purchased in 1954 in St. Louis, Missouri, in a plain brown box.

    MARKS: None

    SEE: *Illustration 409* (front). *(Mary Lou Trowbridge Collection.) Illustration 410* (back). (Mary Lou Trowbridge Collection.) Illustration 411 (panties). *(Mary Lou Trowbridge Collection.)*

Illustration 412.

Illustration 413.

Illustration 414.

Style Show Dolls: HP; 18in (45.7cm); in long dresses; see characteristics of other *Style Show Doll;* circa 1950.

   MARKS: None; silver wrist tag

   SEE: *Illustration 412. (Mary Lou Trowbridge Collection.)* From left to right: (1) *Garden Party;* long flocked printed dress; straw bonnet; yellow ribbon under chin and flowers on bonnet. (2) *Lawn Party;* long dress printed with tiny rosebuds; black sash; cloche type hat with flowers.

Style Show Doll: HP; 18in (45.7cm); see characteristics of other *Style Show Doll;* some collectors believe these school type dresses were sold by Nancy Ann also; white dress with pink and blue hearts; pink hair bows; circa 1950.

   MARKS: None

   SEE: *Illustration 413* (front). *(Mary Lou Trowbridge Collection.) Illustration 414* (back). *(Mary Lou Trowbridge Collection.)*

REFERENCES TO OTHER *STYLE SHOW DOLLS:*—————————
Other *Style Show Dolls* included a "Summer Resort Series." A transitional *Style Show Doll* had a vinyl head with rooted hair, closed mouth and sleep eyes and a HP body.

Illustration 415.

Muffie: HP; 8in (20.3cm); wig of saran or dynel; head turning walker; straight legs (a few came with bent knees); individual fingers; closed mouth; loop arm hook (see Identification Guide; page 263F); painted eyelashes above eye; circa 1953. The early dolls have only painted eyelashes above eyes. Later ones ahve molded lashes. *Muffie* often came in a box with just panties and leather-type shoes and socks. Clothes and accessories were available in the stores.
    MARKS: "Storybook Dolls, California;" box marked: "Playtime Dolls by Nancy Ann, San Francisco, California." Some dolls were marked "Muffie."
    SEE: *Illustration 415.*
    PRICE: $65-95

Illustration 416.

Debbie: vinyl head; HP body; 11in (27.9cm); rooted brown hair; individual fingers; bendable knees; arm hook (see Identification Guide, page 263F); closed mouth; blue sleep eyes; eyelashes; painted eyelashes under eyes; not a walker; pronounced wrist mark on palm side of hand; normal wrist line on back of hand; V-shaped cutout on inner leg; blue pinafore; red striped blouse; red trim. *Debbie* was also made with a HP head; circa 1954.

> **MARKS:** "Nancy Ann" (back of neck); very often the doll is found unmarked because the raised letters easily wear off.
> **SEE:** *Illustration 416.*
> **PRICE:** $35-50

Illustration 417.

Illustration 418.

Lori Ann (girl and boy): HP; 8in (20.3cm); similar to *Muffie*; skin tone rosier; other characteristics the same as *Muffie* including the arm hook (see Identification Guide, page 264G); came undressed in pants, plastic shoes and socks; sleep eyes; closed mouth; turning head walker; painted eyelashes above eyes; single line seat; rare dolls; 1953.

> **MARKS:** None; original box is blue with blue polka dots; the top has printed the words "Lori Ann," and the rest of the box has the traditional "Nancy Ann Story Book Dolls" in script.
> **SEE:** *Illustration 417.*
> **PRICE:** $75-80 girl
> $90-95 boy

Lori Ann: vinyl head; HP body; 7½in (19.1cm); girl has wig; head turning walker; individual fingers; sleep eyes with molded lashes; *Muffie* arm hook (see Identification Guide, page 264G); jointed knees; single line seat; painted lashes above eye; closed mouth; blue dress; straw hat with red band; 1958.

> **MARKS:** "Nancy Ann" (head); "Storybook Dolls, California"
> **SEE:** *Illustration 418.*
> **PRICE:** $25-35

Nᴀᴛᴜʀᴀʟ

DOLLS NOT PHOTOGRAPHED BY AUTHORS:
Bride: HP; 17in (43.2cm); open mouth with four teeth; head turning walker; molded shoes; circa 1952.

> **MARKS:** None; tag "I can walk//Its a Natural."

PEGGY NISBET

Peggy Nisbet began making dolls during the early 1950s. Her first doll was a souvenir type doll made for the coronation of Queen Elizabeth. This doll wore a beautifully sewn outfit and was very popular. This was the beginning of a company which is still producing hard plastic dolls with exquisite and authentic outfits.

The company has grown and suffered through problems such as a major fire, but today the House of Nisbet Ltd., under the direction of Peggy Nisbet's daughter and son-in-law, Alison and Jack Wilson, is producing many, many types and styles of dolls. Just recently the company has produced bisque and vinyl in addition to their hard plastic line.

There are two basic styles of hard plastic dolls. Both are small 7 to 10in (17.8 to 25.4cm), and are made from a one-piece head and body. The first type uses a "dolly" face, and the second type uses a "portrait" face sculpted to look like a famous historical or modern person.

Peggy Nisbet's dolls, made by the House of Nisbet Ltd., portray people and costumes of both past and present. The quality of the costuming is very high with much attention paid to details through various trims, braids, jewelry and fabric selection.

Many of the dolls produced during the 1950s and 1960s are still available today. However, she has made many limited collection series, usually with the portrait dolls, that have been numbered and are highly prized by collectors.

These English dolls can be found all over the world and can be purchased at an affordable price.

Queen Isabella: HP; "dolly face;" 7½in (19.1cm); painted shoes and stockings; one-piece body jointed only at the arms; very slender body; painted eyes; lovely flesh tone; beautifully sewn dress that is orange with brown fur; late 1960s.

MARKS: "Made in England" (back); tag (outside) "Collectors Costume Dolls by Peggy Nisbet, Made in England;" tag (inside) "H/298 Queen Isabella, Consort of Edward II, 1292-1358, Made in England."

SEE: *Illustration 419.*

PRICE: $30-40

Illustration 419.

Illustration 420.

King Henry VIII and *Wives:*

King Henry: HP; "portrait face" made of a different type of hard plastic; 8in (20.3cm); specially molded "fat" body; one-piece body and head jointed only at the arms; authentic costume; painted shoes; painted eyes; red coat with fur trim; white stockings; still available today.

MARKS: wrist tag (inside) "A Peggy Nisbet Modern Royal Miniature Figures, H/218, King Henry VIII, 1491-1547, Made in England."

Henry's Wives: see description of *Queen Isabella;* "dolly faces;" beautifully created costumes. From left to right:

1. *Catherine of Aragon;* purple brocade dress; white fur; black veil.
2. *Anne Boleyn;* blue satin dress; red underskirt; white fur.
3. *Jane Seymour;* pink and blue satin dress and hat; white fur sleeves.
4. *Anne of Cleves;* brown velvet dress; beige lace trim.
5. *Catherine Howard;* black and brown velvet and satin dress.
6. *Catherine Parr;* blue satin dress; gold underskirt; brown fur sleeves.

MARKS: Wrist tags
SEE: *Illustration 420.*
PRICE: $50-55

NOMA
(See Effanbee)

PALITOY-CASCELLOID

In 1919 this company was established in Leicester, England, and they made toys from an early plastic with a celluloid-type base. Later they produced *Kewpie* dolls from this material. They changed their plastic formula several times and by 1940 were making composition dolls with Plastex. After World War II, they turned to a light, shiny HP body with a PH matte head. In 1968 General Mills of America bought the company.

Illustration 421.

Illustration 422.

Bride: HP; 7½in (19.1cm); 2nd and 3rd fingers molded together; unusual purple eyes; one-piece body; jointed at arms only; molded; white satin dress and veil; matching lace trim; painted gray shoes.
    MARKS: "Palitoy/35, Made in England"
    SEE: *Illustration 421.*
    PRICE: $15-20

Scottish Girl: HP; 14in (35.6cm); unusual lighter quality HP; brown sleep eyes with long lashes; blue eye shadow; mohair wig; all fingers except thumb molded together; blue velvet jacket; plaid skirt and matching hat; white lace blouse; green socks.
    MARKS: "Palitoy/35, Made in England"
    SEE: *Illustration 422.*
    PRICE: $75-85

PARADISE WALKING DOLL

Cowboy: HP; 14in (35.6cm); leather wig; dressed like cowboy; carrying a gun.

> **MARKS:** Unknown; marks on box "Paradise Walking Doll Created by Doll's Paradise, N.Y."
>
> **SEE:** *Illustration 423. (Jean Canaday Collection.)*
>
> **PRICE:** $85-105

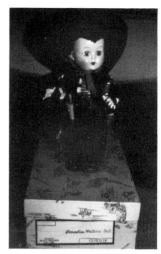

Illustration 423.

PARIS DOLL COMPANY

Girl: HP; 27in (68.6cm); walker; open mouth with teeth; lines above and below dimpled knees. This is a large "bulky" doll with a beautiful skin tone and hair; it can wear little girl dresses. It also came as a majorette.

> **MARKS:** None
>
> **SEE:** *Illustration 424. (Louise Schnell Collection.)*
>
> **PRICE:** $75-100 (dressed)

Illustration 424.

PATTERNS

Home sewing was popular as well as necessary during the 1950s. Everyone was interested in fashion which changed rapidly and radically during the period. Sewing doll clothes from the latest patterns was a hobby for mothers and grandmothers. The sewing machines whirled faster when Christmas approached.

The pictures of popular patterns of the time are included in this book so that the reader might know the clothes of various types of dolls. Copies of old patterns are available. Check various doll magazines for the address of people who will sell the copies.

Illustration 425.

Illustration 426.

Illustration 427.

Butterick Patterns:

   Illustration 425. No. 7565 for Ideal's *Toni, Harriet Hubbard Ayer, Mary Hartline, Princess Mary, Sarah Ann.*
   Illustration 426. No. 7974 for *Sweet Sue* by American Character.
   Illustration 427 for Ideal's *Toni Walker.*

McCall Patterns:

Illustration 428. No. 1561 for Ideal's *Toni*; 1950.

Illustration 429. No. 1646 for Ideal's *Toni*; 1951.

Illustration 430. No. 1653 for *Marcie Doll* and others of same size.

Illustration 431. No. 1728 for Ideal's *Betsy McCall*; 1952.

Illustration 432. No. 1812 for Ideal's *Betsy McCall*, 1953.

Illustration 433. No. 1823 for *Sweet Sue* by American Character.

Illustration 434. No. 1894 for *Betsy McCall* and *Toni* by Ideal; 1954.

Illustration 435. No. 1898 for *Ginny*, Alexander *Wendy-kins*, Nancy Ann *Muffie, Lingerie Lou, Gigi, Daily Dolly*; 1954.

Illustration 436. No. 1965 for Vogue *Ginny*, Alexander *Wendy*, Nancy Ann *Muffie, Lingerie Lou, Gigi, Daily Dolly*; 1955.

Illustration 437. No. 1983 for American Character's *Sweet Sue;* Ideal's *Toni, Harriet Hubbard, Alice, Maggie*; 1955.

Illustration 438. No. 2150 for Vogue *Ginny*, Alexander *Alexander-kins*, Nancy Ann *Muffie, Lingerie Lou, Gigi, Daily Dolly, Mary Lou*; 1957.

Illustration 429.

Illustration 428.

Illustration 430.

Illustration 431.

Illustration 432.

Illustration 433.

Illustration 434.

Illustration 435.

Illustration 436.

Illustration 437.

Illustration 438.

Simplicity Patterns:

Illustration 439. No. 1336 for *Sweet Sue* by American Character.
Illustration 440. No. 1779 for American Character's *Sweet Sue*, Alexander *Binnie.*
Illustration 441. No. 2293 for Uneeda's *Dollikins*, Alexander *Cissy.*
Illustration 442. No. 2745 for Uneeda's *Dollikins*, Alexander *Cissy.*
Illustration 443. No. 3252 for Alexander *Cissy.*
Illustration 444. No. 3728 for Ideal's *Toni.*
Illustration 445. No. 4509 for Ideal's *Bonnie Braids, Saucy Walker.*

Illustration 439.

Illustration 440.

Illustration 441.

Illustration 442.

Illustration 443.

Illustration 444.

Illustration 445.

Lingerie Lou, ready to dress dolls and patterns.
Illustration 446.

Illustration 446.

PEDIGREE SOFT TOYS LTD., LONDON

Pedigree was an English major doll company. They competed with American companies. Two examples were similar versions of Ideal's *Toni* and *Saucy Walker.* They also made *Sindy* which has been a competitor of *Barbie.* Through the years, they have also made many black dolls.

Black girl: HP; 10½in (26.7cm) chubby little girl type; closed mouth; sleep eyes with lashes; wig over molded hair; diamond seat; individually molded fingers with dimples below knuckles; beautiful creamy skin color; wig over molded hair; not in original clothes.
MARKS: "Made in England"
SEE: *Illustration 447.*
PRICE: $15-20

Illustration 447.

DOLLS NOT PHOTOGRAPHED

Pedigree made many other types of dolls. *Shelly Ann* was a *Ginny* look-alike, all-HP, 8in (20.3cm) and marked "Made in England."

Walking all-HP dolls were made in several sizes. A 20in (50.8cm) *Saucy Walker*-type was made marked "Pedigree, England, Pat. Pending." A 12in (30.5cm) walking doll with molded shoes was marked "Pedigree, Made in England."

A *Pin-Up Doll*, all-HP, came with nylon hair and a permanent wave kit. She looked like *Toni.*

PLASTIC MOLDED ARTS
(PMA)

This was a very prolific doll parts company. They made parts for many other companies and sold them far and wide. A few parts are marked, but most of them are not. They were often made in imitation of more expensive dolls and sold well. The quality of the plastic, facial paint, clothes varies greatly.

The dolls that are pictured, and the dolls that are referred to in other books are only a few of the many manufactured. In some cases, the dolls were made by PMA and sold under their label. Other times, the same dolls dressed exactly the same were marketed by another company (see TV Cowboy listed under A & H). Dolls were produced between 1949 and 1955.

PMA IDENTIFICATION:

Because many PMA dolls are not marked, and because PMA sold dolls to many other companies, all pictured doll body parts in the Identification Guide are from marked dolls unless otherwise noted. Features such as arm hooks, molded shoes, eyelashes, and mouth are shown in the Identification Guide for quick help in the identification of other dolls.

The smaller less expensive 5 to 10in (12.7 to 25.4cm) fall into two main categories. They are as follows:

1. PMA
2. Beehler Arts-Ontario Plastics.

Refer to these companies for identification features of their dolls. It is quite easy, with practice, to quickly distinguish between the two.

PMA CHARACTERISTICS:

1. Double triangle mouth.
2. Molded eyelashes.
3. Heavy eyelashes beneath eyes.
4. Ear mold runs through ear.
5. 2nd and 3rd fingers molded together.
6. Two lines on palm of hand.
7. The tiny early dolls often have eyelashes above eye and no molded or imitation eyelashes.
8. The great majority have sleep eyes.
9. Most of the dolls have the standard arm hook (see Identification Guide, page 264H).
10. Molded and painted shoes with bow detail. There are several different types (see Identification Guide, pages 283A, B, C) for details on shoes.

   SEE: *Illustration 448* (double triangle mouth).

Illustration 448.

Illustration 449.

Illustration 450.

Illustration 451.

Illustration 452.

Illustration 453.

Girl: HP; 10in (25.4cm); PMA characteristics; additional features include eyebrows slightly pointed; circle mold flaw on upper arms; two lines under nose; excellent quality plastic; fully-jointed; regular toe detail; blue formal faded to gray.
MARKS: "PMA" (lower back)
SEE: *Illustration 449.*
PRICE: $10-20

Girl: HP; 10in (25.4cm); PMA characteristics; one-piece body and legs; molded on white shoes; circle flaw on upper arms; two lines under nose; dimples on each side of knees; gray and pink taffeta dress; pink sash.
MARKS: "Plastic Molded Arts L.I.C. N.Y." (back)
SEE: *Illustration 450. (Pat Parton Collection.)*
PRICE: $10-20 (each)

TV Cowboy: HP; 7in (17.8cm); this is the exact same doll labeled Marcie TV Cowboy found in the A & H section; white and green leather outfit. The Marcie doll is unmarked.
MARKS: "Plastic Molded Arts Co. L.I.C. New York" (back)
SEE: *Illustration 451.*
PRICE: $25-30

Indian: HP; unusual doll; side glancing eyes; painted on shoes (see Identification Guide, page 283C); Indian scalp haircut; molded T-strap shoes painted white with a series of dots on toes (see Identification Guide, page 283C); brown, white and red woven blanket.
MARKS: "Plastic Molded Arts L.I.C. N.Y." (back)
SEE: *Illustration 452. (Phyllis Appell Collection.)*
PRICE: $5-10

Irish dolls: same doll except for size; PMA characteristics; green shamrocks on their skirts, white satin skirts; green ribbon tops; painted on shoes (see Identification Guide, A).
MARKS: Doll on left: 6in (15.2cm) "Plastic Molded Arts Co. L.I.C. N.Y." (back). Doll on right: 7½in (19.1cm); no marks.
SEE: *Illustration 453.*
PRICE: $5-10 (each)

Hawaiian Girl: HP; 15in (38.1cm); excellent quality brownish plastic; well made and similar to *Haleloke*; individual fingers; dark flesh tone; regular walker; head turns; open mouth; two teeth; feathered eyebrows; green skirt; yellow lei.

MARKS: "Plastic Molded Arts L.I.C. N.Y." (back)

SEE: *Illustration 454. (Sandy Strater Collection.)*

PRICE: $25-40

Girl: HP; 5in (12.7cm); wearing red dress; similar to the Indian; also similar to Knickerbocker, Reliable, and S & E dolls; molded painted hair; shoes same as Indian (see Identification Guide, page 283C); red print dress with a yellow ribbon.

MARKS: "Plastic Molded Arts, L.I.C. N.Y." (back)

SEE: *Illustration 455. (Marie Ezzo Collection.)*

PRICE: $5-10

DOLLS WITH NO MARKS, BUT ATTRIBUTED TO PMA

Captain Hook: HP; 7½in (19.1cm); right arm is a hook, PMA characteristics with mustache and eyebrows painted on; painted high boots (see Identification Guide, page 283A for pictures of shoes with bows); black suit and hat; red belt; black feather in hat.

MARKS: None

SEE: *Illustration 456. (Marie Ezzo Collection.)*

PRICE: $25-30

Illustration 454.

Illustration 455.

Illustration 456.

Illustration 457.

Miss Valentine: HP; 7in (17.8cm); PMA characteristics; one-piece body and legs; white satin skirt; red Valentines; red and white ribbon bodice. An interesting note was pinned to her slip underneath her dress. It says "Bonnie from Nani, February, 1953."

MARKS: "#2" (right arm); "#1" (left arm); none on body

SEE: *Illustration 457.*

PRICE: $10-15

Illustration 459.

Illustration 458.

High Heeled Girl: HP; 7½in (19.1cm); PMA characteristics; plastic bra and pants; see also Doll Bodies.
    MARKS: None
    SEE: *Illustration 458* (doll). *Illustration 459* (bra). *Illustration 460* (back of bra).
    PRICE: $5-10

Miss America: HP; 7½in (19.1cm); PMA characteristics; PMA shoes (see Identification Guide, page 283B); red striped taffeta skirt; blue sash; white bodice with red trim.
    MARKS: None
    SEE: *Illustration 461.*
    PRICE: $5-10

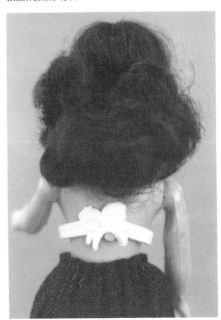

Illustration 460.

UNKNOWN DOLLS WITH PMA CHARACTERISTICS:

Martha Washington-type: HP; 10½in (26.7cm); PMA characteristics; PMA shoes (see Identification Guide, page 283B).
MARKS: None
SEE: *Illustration 462. (Phyllis Appell Collection.)*
PRICE: $10-15

Girl: HP; 12in (30.5cm); excellent quality plastic with beautiful glossy hair; PMA characteristics; painted-on shoes with bows that are so worn they cannot be identified; mold marks on upper arms; pin jointed walker with painted countersunk screw for pin; pink nylon dress.
MARKS: None
SEE: *Illustration 463.*
PRICE: $25-35

Queen: HP; 11in (27.9cm); PMA characteristics; molded toes; flaw mark on upper arm; two dimples on each side of knee; silver dress and overskirt; purple ribbon with jewels.
MARKS: None
SEE: *Illustration 464.*
PRICE: $10-15

Long John Silver: HP; 7½in (19.1cm); wooden leg; PMA characteristics; patch on eye; black shirt; red belt; white pants.
MARKS: None
SEE: *Illustration 465. (Phyllis Appell Collection.)*
PRICE: $25-30

Illustration 461.

Illustration 463.

Illustration 462.

Illustration 464.

Illustration 465.

DOLLS NOT PHOTOGRAPHED BY AUTHORS:

Along with production of 1950 fashion dolls and regular walking dolls, Plastic Molded Arts made a small *Ginny*-type doll. One was about 7½in (10.1cm) and called *Petite Cheri*. She was a HP walker with a head that turned and pin joints on her legs. This doll also came in a 10in (25.4cm) chubby size. There are no marks on the doll.

Vicki was a 7½in (10.1cm) all-HP walking doll with molded on T-strap shoes. She later had a vinyl head and a HP body. Both were sometimes marked "Vicki" but often were unmarked.

PLAYHOUSE DOLLS

Illustration 466.

Priest and Nun: HP; 7½in (19.1cm); both with Plastic Molded Arts characteristics (see PMA); Marcie doll folder in box (see A & H); PMA shoes (see Identification Guide, page 283B); the priest is exactly like the priest described in the A & H Marcie section except that he does not have a label in his cassock; black with white satin and lace. Nun in all white.

> **MARKS:** None on body; box "Play-House Dolls//Jaret & Diamond//401 Broadway, N.Y. City."
> **SEE:** *Illustration 466.*
> **PRICE:** $10-15 each

Little Red Riding Hood: HP; 7½in (19.1cm); Virga-type characteristics (see Virga); painted side glancing eyes; Virga shoes; red cape; red checked apron; white dress; straw basket.

> **MARKS:** None on doll; box "Play-House Dolls//Jaret & Diamond//401 Broadway, N.Y. City."
> **SEE:** *Illustration 467.*
> **PRICE:** $10-15

Illustration 467.

RAVON

(See Artisan Novelty Co.)

Ravon made a *Raving Beauty* doll. She was all HP, 18½in (47cm) with a red wig; circa 1951. There are no marks on the doll but the box is marked "Raving Beauty."

RELIABLE

(Canada)

Illustration 468.

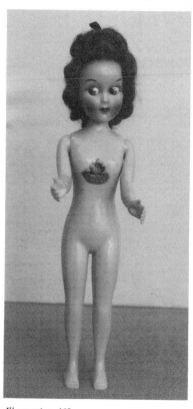

Illustration 469.

Eskimo: HP; 6in (15.2cm); simulated fur and yellow leather suit.
    MARKS: "Reliable, Made in Canada"
    SEE: *Illustration 468. (Phyllis Appell Collection.)*
    PRICE: $8-10

Mapleleaf Girl: HP; 7in (17.8cm); jointed at arms and neck only; sleep eyes; slender body.
    MARKS: "Mapleleaf" (front of body); "Montreal, Canada"
    SEE: *Illustration 469. (Phyllis Appell Collection.)*
    PRICE: $8-10

Illustration 470.

Little Girl: HP; 6in (15.2cm); crocheted dress; Knickerbocker look-alike; side glancing eyes; gauntlet hands; jointed only at arms and neck; Knickerbocker-type painted on socks and shoes (see Identification Guide, page 286L); crocheted varigated yellow and pink dress.

MARKS: "Reliable" (cursive writing); "Made in Canada"

SEE: *Illustration 470.*

PRICE: $8-10

RENWAL DOLL HOUSE DOLLS

Miniature "people" for doll houses have delighted children and adults for many generations. In the late 1940s and 1950s, the Renwal Company made shiny, hard plastic, painted dolls that stood well and wore molded-on clothes. The toddlers were fully jointed, and the "Family" dolls could sit and kneel as well as stand.

Today these well played with figures are scarce, and to find them mint in box is very rare. Most collectors are happy to find them in any condition.

The company also made excellent furniture with functioning doors, drawers, mirrors, and others. The dolls and furniture reflect the "Fabulous Fifties," and the desire of families to have nice homes and well cared for children in the suburbs.

Illustration 471.

Family 1940s and early 1950s from left to right:
1. Brother; 3⅝in (9.2cm); blue suit. **PRICE:** $15-20
2. Mother; 4⅛in (10.5cm); red dress. **PRICE:** $15-20
3. Father; 4¼in (10.8cm); black suit. **PRICE:** $15-20
4. Doctor; 4¼in (10.8cm); white uniform. **PRICE:** $20-25
5. Sister; 3½in (8.9cm); yellow dress. **PRICE:** $15-20
6. Nurse; 4⅛in (10.5cm); white uniform. **PRICE:** $20-25

SEE: *Illustration 471. (Helen Kirschnick Collection.)*

Large toddler: HP; 5in (12.7cm) (not a miniature); molded white shirt and blue pants; 1940s and early 1950s.
SEE: *Illustration 472. (Helen Kirschnick Collection.)*
PRICE: $10-15

Illustration 472.

RICHWOOD TOYS

Richwood Toys of Annapolis, Maryland, produced an excellent quality hard plastic walking doll with an extensive line of clothes including street wear, formal wear and sports clothes. The doll is similar to *Betsy McCall* with a thin, delicate body. Today it is rare and commands high prices for such a small 8in (20.3cm) doll.

The head of this doll does not turn when she walks, and the model was made with both flat and high heeled feet. The eyebrows and eyelashes below the sleep eyes are an unusual dark orange color which can help with the identification.

Illustration 473.

Illustration 473a.

Sandra Sue: 8in (20.3cm); walker; head does not turn; sleep eyes; highly arched, thin, dark orange eyebrows and eyelashes below the eyes; closed mouth; thin legs; high heeled feet; 1st, 2nd and 3rd fingers molded together; ♀ on the backside; loop arm hook (see Identification Guide, page 263F); white net skirt with red velvet bodice and red velvet flowers on the skirt; circa 1956.

 MARKS: "3" (inside of right arm); backward "3" (left arm)
 SEE: *Illustration 473.*
 PRICE: $80

Sandra Sue: 8in (20.3cm); walker; head does not turn; sleep eyes; highly arched, thin, dark orange eyebrows and eyelashes below the eyes; closed mouth; thin legs; high heeled feet; 1st, 2nd and 3rd fingers molded together; ♀ on backside; black street dress with pink trim and hat; circa 1956.

 MARKS: "3" (inside of right arm); backward "3" (left arm)
 SEE: *Illustration 473a. (Pat Parton Collection.)*
 PRICE: $80

Sandra Sue: 8in (20.3cm); walker;
head does not turn; sleep eyes; highly
arched, thin, dark orange eyebrows
and eyelashes below the eyes; closed
mouth; thin legs; flat feet; 1st, 2nd and
3rd fingers molded together; ○
on the backside; red ski pants and hat
and green top with trim; circa 1956.
> **MARKS:** "2" (inside of right
> arm); "0" inside of left arm
> **SEE:** *Illustration 473b.*
> **PRICE:** $80

Illustration 473b.

R OBERTA

The Roberta Doll Company has a history of selling dolls with very uneven
quality. Both the dolls and the clothes have many variations. Many of their dolls were
mass copies of more expensive dolls. However, some dolls have lovely flesh tones and
very pretty features.

The company also made personality dolls such as *LuAnn Simms* and *Haleloke*
which seem to have a very different, more expensive quality from some of their other
line.

Girl: HP; 14in (35.6cm); very slim
body; very pretty face; heavy eyeshadow in unusual grey shade; very
dark eyebrows; heavy makeup; sleep
eyes with lashes; lashes painted under
eyes; pretty flesh tone; pin jointed
walker; head turns; prong arm hook
(see Identification Guide, page 265J);
closed mouth; 2nd and 3rd fingers
molded together; little finger slightly
molded backward; rivet type leg pin
(see Identification Guide, page 290C);
pink and gray dress; pink ribbon;
circa 1951.
> **MARKS:** "Made in U.S.A." (in
> circle on back)
> **SEE:** *Illustration 474* (doll). *Il-
> lustation 475* (close-up). *Illus-
> tration 476* (markings).
> **PRICE:** $45-55

Illustration 474.

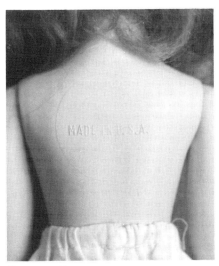

Illustration 475.

Illustration 476.

Illustration 477.

Roberta Walker: HP; 8½in (21.6cm); head turning walker; molded hair under wig; countersunk painted hip pin; excellent detail on fingers and toes; individually molded fingers; unusual knee dimple with two lines underneath; standard arm hook (see Identification Guide, page 2641); red checked dress; red and white braid trim; circa 1951.

MARKS: None
SEE: *Illustration 477. (Pat Parton Collection.)*
PRICE: $15-25

Illustration 478.   *Illustration 479.*

Illustration 480.

Girl (*Ginny*-type) (see Doll Bodies Products): HP; 7in (17.8cm); non-walker; molded and painted shoes with bows in front (see Identification Guide, page 286K); fatter legs than most of the *Ginny* look-alike dolls; molded eyelashes; eyelashes painted faintly under eye; individual fingers on left hand; 2nd and 3rd fingers molded together slightly; made a boy version called *Johnny*; circa 1952 to 1953.

    MARKS: None; some have "Doll Bodies Products" (back)

    SEE: *Illustration 478*. Red bodice; multi-colored skirt. *Illustration 479*. White dress with multi-colored print; blue rickrack trim. *(Pat Parton Collection.)*

    PRICE: $15-25

Lu Ann Simms: (see Horsman for description; see also Valentine); this doll has been identified with a Roberta label. Both the Roberta version and the Valentine version have characteristics of the Horsman dolls. During the 1950s, it was common for distributing companies to buy and dress dolls from other companies (see detailed description, pages 108 and 237).

    MARKS: "180"

    SEE: *Illustration 480*. Center and right doll. *(Pat Parton Collection.)*

    PRICE: $55-75

R<u>ODDY</u>

(D. G. Todd & Company Ltd., England)

The trademark "Roddy" was used by Daniel G. Todd, managing director of Toy Time Toys Ltd. of Lancashire, England, about 1948. They were making an all-plastic injection-molded doll.

Three dolls with different faces; the Roddy Dolls featured an unusual neck action with their walking dolls. The doll in the middle has her neck akimbo which was one stage in the walking action. 1951.

MARKS: "Roddy, Made in England" (back)

SEE: *Illustration 481. (Rosemary Romance Collection.)*

Girl: HP; 12in (30.5cm); fluttery sleep eyes; head attached to rod and head moves from side to side in unusual manner when the doll walks; clenched hands; original clothes and label; pink print dress; blue trim; circa 1951.

MARKS: "Roddy, Made in England" (back)

SEE: *Illustration 482* (doll). *(Mary Jane Poley Collection.) Illustration 483* (label). *(Mary Jane Poley Collection.) Illustration 484* (label). *(Mary Jane Poley Collection.)*

PRICE: $35-45

Illustration 481.

Illustration 482.

Illustration 483.

Illustration 484.

Girl: HP; 12½in (31.8cm); wig; open mouth; two teeth; molded tongue; fluttery sleep eyes with lashes; molded on slipper shoes; individual fingers; unusual tilt to head in walking movement; plaid dress; white blouse; circa 1951.
MARKS: "Roddy, Made in England" (back)
SEE: *Illustration 485.*
PRICE: $35-45

Boy: HP; 12in (30.5cm); open mouth; two teeth; concealed pin joint walker (see Identification Guide; page 291D); 1951
MARKS: "Roddy, Made in England" (back)
SEE: *Illustration 486. (Laura Brown Collection.)*
PRICE: $30-40

German Girl: HP; 7½in (19.1cm); *Ginny* look-alike; head turning walker; 2nd and 3rd fingers molded together; shoes say, "Made in England;" standard arm hook (see Identification Guide, page 264H); blue skirt; white blouse; red embroidered bodice; red scarf and hat; circa 1951.
MARKS: "Roddy" (cursive writing), "Made in England" (back)
SEE: *Illustration 487.*
PRICE: $25-30

Girl: HP; 9in (22.9cm); molded white clothes; sleep eyes with molded lashes; head turning walker; very unusual arm action; joints open outward from below the sleeve of the dress; individual fingers facing the body; molded shoes and socks; closed mouth; circa 1951.
MARKS: "Roddy, Made in England" (back)
SEE: *Illustration 488. (Thelma Purvis Collection.)*
PRICE: $10-20

Illustration 485.

Illustration 487.

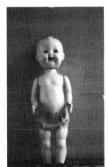

Illustration 486.

Illustration 488.

ROSALIE
(Manufacturer Unknown)

Girl: HP; 7in (17.8cm); one-piece stout body and legs; jointed arms; standard arm hook; closed mouth; sleep eyes; painted on eyelashes on head itself; no molded eyelashes; four fingers molded together; painted on shoes over molded shoes (see Identification Guide, page 285H); many Virga, Fortune characteristics; one single line crease on seat; red skirt; black veil; black bodice; black lace trim with gold rickrack.

MARKS: None; on box "A Rosalie Doll"
SEE: *Illustration 489.*

PRICE: $10-15

Brochure (found with girl): brochure lists the following types of Rosalie dolls:

Bridesmaid Green
Bridesmaid Blue
Bridesmaid Gold
Bridegroom
June Bride
Red Riding Hood
Sweet Sixteen
Bridesmaid Pink
Colored Mammy
Farmerette
Little Bo Peep
Carmen
Dutch Maid
Scotch Lassie
Italian Girl
Nun in White
Nurse
Nun in Black

Illustration 489.

SEE: *Illustration 490* (brochure). *Illustration 491* (brochure).

Illustration 490.

Illustration 491.

ROSEBUD
(England)

DOLLS NOT PHOTOGRAPHED

In 1947 Eric Smith of Raunds, Northampton, registered the trademark, "Rosebud #657461," for dolls. His HP production included:

1. A painted 6in (15.2cm) molded hair baby with sleep eyes. She was marked "Rosebud, Made in England."
2. A 21in (53.3cm) girl with a vinyl head and HP body, closed mouth, two painted teeth and a pull string talking device. She speaks with an English accent.
3. A HP 7in (17.8cm) tourist-type doll with sleep eyes and molded shoes.
4. A 10in (25.4cm) boy with painted hair, sleep eyes and a closed mouth. He is marked "Rosebud" on his head, and "Rosebud, Made in England, Pat. #667906" on his body.
5. A 15in (38.1cm) all HP head turning walker with a wig, open/closed mouth with two teeth.

S & E

Illustration 492.

Girl: HP; 5½in (14cm); painted side glancing eyes; red dots in nose; bow mouth; one-piece body including head; molded painted shoes and socks (see Identification Guide, page 286L); mitten hands; yellow cotton dotted dress; white lace trim at hem line; yellow ribbons; circa 1952 to 1953.
   MARKS: "S & E" (body)
   SEE: *Illustration 492. (Pat Parton Collection.)*
   PRICE: $8-12

Girl: HP; 5½in (14cm); green dress with yellow scarf; same characteristics as other S & E girl; circa 1952 to 1953.
   MARKS: "S & E" (body)
   SEE: *Illustration 493. (Ann Lotterman Collection.)*
   PRICE: $8-12

Illustration 493.

SAYCO

Like many of the "popular priced" doll firms, Sayco made many dolls during the 1950s. For the most part, they "met" the competition, and their dolls and wardrobes were eagerly purchased. Glamour dolls such as the Miss America Pageant doll and airline stewardess doll were very popular. The stewardess came in a uniform with a shoulder bag.

Bride: vinyl head; HP body; 28in (71.1cm); pin jointed walker; closed mouth; sleep eyes; individual fingers; white satin dress with lace; circa 1956.

MARKS: "Sayco 750;" or none

SEE: *Illustration 494* (doll). *(Pat Parton Collection.) Illustration 495* (close-up). *(Pat Parton Collection.)*

PRICE: $25-40

Illustration 494.

Illustration 495.

UNKNOWN WITH SAYCO CHARACTERISTICS:

Girl (left): vinyl head; HP body; 20in (50.8cm); individual fingers; pin-jointed head turning walker with rivet pin (see Identification Guide, page 290C); sleep eyes with lashes; very pretty hair; painted eyelashes under eyes; closed mouth; circa 1956. See page 224 for description of bride.

MARKS: "AE"
SEE: *Illustration 496.*
PRICE: $25-40

DOLLS NOT PHOTOGRAPHED

Miss America Pageant: HP; 8in (20.3cm); similar to *Ginny*; 50 all occasions ensembles including TWA stewardess complete with shoulder bag; circa 1956.

MARKS: Unknown

Playgirl-Baby: HP head; cloth body; latex arms and legs; sleep eyes; two teeth; circa 1950.

MARKS: "Made in USA/750" (head); "Sayco" (box)

Girl: HP; vinyl head; 17in (43.2cm); rooted hair; closed mouth; sleep eyes; circa 1956.

MARKS: "Sayco" (head)

Illustration 496.

STAR

(Also see Desota)

DOLLS NOT PHOTOGRAPHED

Dorothy Collins: HP; 14in (35.6cm); glued on yellow hair; blue sleep eyes; head turning walker; open mouth; circa 1954.

MARKS: "14" (head); "Made in USA" (back)

STARR

Starr made a HP 7½in (19.1cm) doll with a closed mouth and sleep eyes during the early 1950s. *Miss Christmas* and *Cowgirl Annie* were part of a series. Most were unmarked, but could have a "7/3" on the head.

TERRI LEE

Violet Gradwohl had a dream. She wanted a baby doll that would be uncomplicated and trigger the imagination of a child. Most of all it must be indestructible.

Unlike other dreamers, she saw her dream grow to reality, and many children in the late 1940s and early 1950s treasured their *Terri Lee* dolls.

However, she did see her dream shatter as fires, court litigation and other problems forced the end of manufacturing. She had sold the dolls with a guarantee that they could be returned for repair to the factory free of charge. It was really an impossible dream.

Thirty years ago little girls adored the unusual doll and the expensive, colorful wardrobe that could be purchased. Mothers also adored the bright, beautiful clothes.

Today a new generation of girls who are fortunate enough to have a mother who saved her doll are dressing and redressing the "almost" indestructible dolls. Each holiday and new season sees a change in the *Terri Lee* doll displayed lovingly in a prominent place in the house.

Early plastic:

Terri Lee was made with two types of material. The first was an early hard plastic. The dolls were marked "Terri Lee, Pat. Pending." Later the doll was made with the more traditional hard plastic. It was marked "Terri Lee," and they were made in the late 1940s and early 1950s.

Terri Lee: early HP or regular HP; 16in (40.6cm); glued on wig of various colors; distinctive features and eyes which were painted; very heavy doll; many clothes available that were all well made; red dots painted in nose like old China dolls; thicker lips than the Mary Jane look-alike; four fingers molded together with separate thumb; single line on seat.
PRICE: $150-175

Jerri Lee: HP; 16in (40.6cm); caracul or fur wig; painted features; same distinctive facial expression as *Terri*; early 1950s.
    SEE: *Illustration 497* (nurse); white uniform. *Illustration 498;* green velvet coat with white felt gloves and boots. *Illustration 499; Terri* is wearing a pink Easter outfit with a straw hat; *Jerri* is wearing a turquoise suit and brown boots. *Illustration 500. (Sandy Strater Collection.) Terri* is wearing a blue print beach outfit with matching bonnet; *Jerri* is wearing blue shorts with a white shirt.
PRICE: $125-150

Tiny Terri: HP; 10in (25.4cm); head turning walker; wig; brown sleep eyes; painted distinctive features that are identified with *Terri Lee*; 1st, 2nd, 3rd fingers molded together; 1956.
    MARKS: "C" (in circle on back)
    SEE: *Illustration 501* (box, tag and doll). *(Sandy Strater Collection.) Illustration 502* (play dress). *Illustration 503* (shorts outfit). *Illustration 504* (clown costume).
PRICE: $90-110

Illustration 497.

Illustration 500.

Illustration 498.

Illustration 501.

Illustration 499.

Illustration 502.

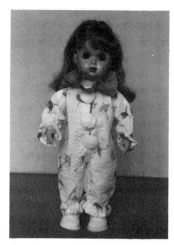

Illustration 503.

Illustration 504.

Illustration 505.

Illustration 506.

Connie Lynn: HP; 19in (48.3cm); glued on red/brown fur hair; sleep eyes; open/closed mouth; curled toes; distinctive facial characteristics of *Terri Lee* family; circa 1956.
MARKS: None
SEE: *Illustration 505. (Ann Lotterman Collection.)*
PRICE: $275-300

Bonnie Lu (black *Terri Lee*): HP; 16in (40.6cm); wig; sleep eyes; same distinctive characteristics of *Terri Lee;* red plaid skirt; red blouse.
MARKS: "Terri Lee"
SEE: *Illustration 506. (Rosemary Romance Collection.)*
PRICE: $350-375

DOLLS NOT PHOTOGRAPHED

Tiny Jerri Lee: HP; 10in (25.4cm); glued on dark fur wig; brown sleep eyes; unusual long lashes; head turning walker; painted features; same characteristics as *Tiny Terri Lee.*

    MARKS: "C" (in circle on back)

Talking Terri Lee: HP and vinyl; doll could be plugged into record player; distinctive features like *Terri Lee.*

    MARKS: "Terri Lee" (back)

Gene Autry: HP; 16in (40.6cm); painted brown hair and eyebrows; decal blue eyes; painted teeth.

    MARKS: "Terri Lee, Pat. Pending" (back)

Benji: HP; black *Jerri Lee*; lamb's wool wig; sleep eyes.

    MARKS: "Terri Lee" (back)

TOGS AND DOLLS

Illustration 507.

Illustration 508.

Penny Walker: HP; 12in (30.5cm); glued on wig; chubby body; sleep eyes with lashes; walker with turning head; eyelashes painted under eyes; dimples in knees; knees very pronounced and heavy; closed mouth; not original arms or clothes; early 1950s.

    MARKS: "Pat. Pend." (head); "Penny Walker" (tag)
    SEE: *Illustration 507.*
    PRICE: $25-35

Twins (Boy and Girl): HP; 12in (30.5cm); glued on wig over molded hair; chubby body; sleep eyes; heavy black eyelashes painted under eyes; dimples in knees; knees are very pronounced and heavy; closed mouth; youthful breast with pronounced nipple on left side; mold flaw at bottom; head turning walker; individual fingers; arm hook (see Identification Guide, page 267T); girl is wearing red checked dress; boy is wearing red shorts and red striped shirt; early 1950s.

    MARKS: "Pat. Pending."
    SEE: *Illustration 508. (Pat Parton Collection.)*
    PRICE: $25-35 each

Illustration 509.

Girl Walker: HP; 10in (25.4cm); glued on wig over molded hair; chubby body; sleep eyes with lashes; heavy black eyelashes painted under eyes; very rounded knees in front with unusual lines on back of knees, especially left knee; individual fingers with dimples below fingers; wrist line around entire wrist; right arm with metal hook around a center HP bar. Left arm has same central bar with normal walker "stop" which prevents doll's arm from going above shoulder; turquoise striped and red dotted dress; early 1950s.

MARKS: None
SEE: *Illustration 509.*
PRICE: $20-30

DOLLS NOT PHOTOGRAPHED

Mary Jane: HP; 17in (43.2cm); vinyl head; head turning walker; arms raise only to shoulder; closed mouth; large "staring" eyes; large mouth.

MARKS: None; wrist tag

UNEEDA

Uneeda has made a line of unusual, collectible dolls since before 1920. These included boy dolls, character babies, toddlers and pretty girl dolls.

With the advent of hard plastic, Uneeda continued to make unusual dolls. One of the best of the era is *Dollikins* with a vinyl head and hard plastic body. It is one of the most fully-jointed hard plastic dolls ever made. Her adult body is graceful, and she is very posable for the 1950s fashions or for ballerina costumes; circa 1957. Later *Dollikins* dolls were made of vinyl. There was also an unusual jointed baby.

MARKS: "Uneeda 2 S" (head)
SEE: *Illustration 510.* The doll on the left has original clothes; blue skirt; red striped blouse. The doll on the right has a replica of a costume worn by the ballerina, Pavlova, made by the owner.
PRICE: $35-50

Illustration 510.

Illustration 511.

Illustration 512.

Illustration 513.

Dollikins: vinyl head; HP; 19in (48.3cm); jointed upper arms (see Identification Guide, page 268W); jointed elbows, shoulders, wrists, hips, knees, ankles; sleep eyes with lashes; pierced ears; fingernail polish; closed mouth; 2nd and 3rd fingers molded together; glossy painted lips; tiny painted eyelashes under eyes; 1957.
MARKS: "Uneeda 2 S"
SEE: *Illustration 511* (undressed doll).
PRICE: $35-50

Janie: vinyl head; HP; *Ginny* look-alike; 8in (20.3cm); large navel; 2nd and 3rd fingers molded together; molded eyelashes; painted eyelashes with three lines at ends of eyes; stubby nose; foot detail sparse; back of foot looks like shoe seams; double crease at ankle; blue checked dress; red bow. Some with pin jointed walker; others not; circa 1955.
MARKS: "U;" or none
SEE: *Illustration 512. (Pat Parton Collection.)*
PRICE: $15-25

Girl: vinyl head; HP body; 21in (53.3cm); closed mouth; sleep eyes with lashes; painted lashes under eyes; rooted hair; spring joint on regular walker legs; jointed knees; Ϋ on seat; individual fingers; pink checked taffeta dress; circa 1955.
MARKS: "Uneeda" (head); "210" (body)
SEE: *Illustration 513. (Pat Parton Collection.)*
PRICE: $30-45

Illustration 514.

Illustration 515.

Illustration 515a.

Illustration 516.

Needa Toddles: HP head; 25in (63.5cm); composition upper arms and legs; wired on arms and legs of early vinyl; screw in center of body for walking apparatus; open mouth with two teeth; dimples on knees and cheeks; early 1950s.

MARKS: "20" (head)
SEE: *Illustration 514* (head). *(Ruth Glover Collection.)* *Illustration 515* (doll). *(Jean Canaday Collection.)*
PRICE: $75-90

Boy *(Janie):* vinyl head; HP; same characteristics as *Janie;* black suit; circa 1955.
MARKS: None
SEE: *Illustration 515a. (Marie Ezzo Collection.)*
PRICE: $15-25

UNKNOWN DOLLS WITH UNEEDA CHARACTERISTICS:_____

Girl: vinyl head; HP; rooted hair; high heeled feet; not jointed at ankle; closed mouth with glossy lips; pronounced oval eyes; tiny painted eyelashes under eyes; individual fingers with dimples under fingers; round arm joint; navel is a depression with no dot in center; individual fingers; red velvet dress with full skirt and tight waist.
MARKS: None
SEE: *Illustration 516. (Mary Beth Manchook Collection.)*
PRICE: $35-45

DOLLS NOT PHOTOGRAPHED

Baby Dollikins: vinyl head; HP; 21in (53.3cm); molded painted hair; sleep eyes; drink and wet mouth; jointed at hips, knees, elbow, shoulders, neck, wrists; circa 1960.
MARKS: "B. Uneeda Doll Co., Inc."

Country Girl: vinyl head with rooted hair; HP; 22in (55.9cm); flirty eyes with lashes; open/closed; saucy walker type; circa 1956.

Toddles: vinyl head/arms/legs; HP body and upper leg; rooted blonde hair; sleep eyes; open/closed mouth; in tummy position; legs locked in kick position; circa 1952.
MARKS: "A" (neck)

UNIQUE

Undressed doll for home sewing:
HP; 8in (20.3cm); sleep eyes but no
lashes; lashes painted on; shoes (see
Identification Guide, page 284D);
shoes the same as for *Lingerie Lou;*
2nd and 3rd fingers molded together.
>MARKS: None
>SEE: *Illustration 517. (Pat Par-
>ton Collection.)*
>PRICE: $5

Illustration 517.

UNKNOWN

When the authors started writing this book, there were many pictures of unknown
dolls. Most are now identified. However, some are left to arouse your curiosity.
Hopefully, someone will identify these dolls and add to our knowledge. No prices are
given.

Baby: HP; 7½in (19.1cm); shiny
plastic; jointed at arms and legs but
not at neck; closed mouth; sleep eyes;
molded eyelashes; two curved lines
under breast; mold line does not cross
over the ear; 2nd and 3rd fingers
molded together; beautiful molded,
painted hair with gentle curls around
head; Nancy Ann's *Muffie*-type of
arm hook (see Identification Guide,
page 263F); dimples in knees; closed
mouth.
>MARKS: None
>SEE: *Illustration 518. (Pat Par-
>ton Collection.)*

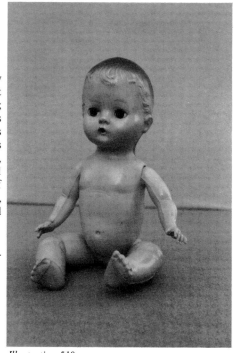

Illustration 518.

High Heeled Doll: HP; 8½in (21.6cm); standard arm hook for fashion dolls (see Identification Guide, page 264H); sleep eyes with molded lashes; PMA mouth; unusual short legs with painted, molded high heel shoes; closed mouth; black strapless formal.

MARKS: None

SEE: *Illustration 519. (Thelma Purvis Collection.) Illustration 520* (feet). *(Thelma Purvis Collection.)*

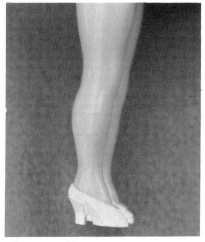

Illustration 519.

Illustration 520.

***Ginny*-type Walker:** this doll is unusual because of the jointed elbows; HP; 8in (20.3cm); jointed knees; closed mouth.

MARKS: None

SEE: *Illustration 521. (Helen Kirschnick Collection.)*

Illustration 521.

Baby Heads: very different hard plastic; both have the same molded painted hair; felt tongue; two teeth. These are possibly Horsman dolls.

> **MARKS:** "350"
> **SEE:** *Illustration 522. (Ruth Glover Collection.) Illustration 523. (Phyllis Appell Collection.)*

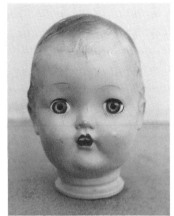

Illustration 522.   *Illustration 523.*

Baby: HP head; cloth body; molded, painted hair only slightly waved and brushed to one side.

> **MARKS:** "550"
> **SEE:** *Illustration 524. (Beatrice Campbell Collection.)*

New Born Baby: unusual head which was placed on a magic skin body; felt tongue.

> **MARKS:** Small "c" on back of head
> **SEE:** *Illustration 525. (Phyllis Appell Collection.)*

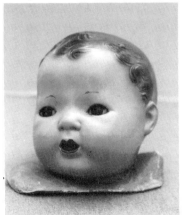

Illustration 524.   *Illustration 525.*

Hawaiian Girl: beautiful HP; doll in box mailed from Hawaii; different from Haleoke and PMA Hawaiian girl; 14in (35.6cm); open mouth with two teeth; grass skirt; yellow top.

    MARKS: None

    SEE: *Illustration 526. (Barbara Schieve Collection.) Illustration 527* (close-up). *(Barbara Schieve Collection.)*

Illustration 526.

Illustration 527.

Majorette: waxy HP; 9in (22.9cm); jointed only at arms; closed mouth; 2nd and 3rd fingers molded together; molded, painted shoes and socks; painted side glancing eyes; molded hair underneath a mohair wig; chubby type body; white satin costume; red trim.

    MARKS: None

    SEE: *Illustration 528.*

Illustration 528.

Valentine

Valentine made many dolls which have become very collectible. They, too, served the mass market, and they made dolls in many price ranges. These dolls include:
Hard plastic personality dolls:
1. *Roxanne,* the hostess of "Beat the Clock," TV show.
2. *Lu Ann Simms,* singer on Arthur Godfrey's TV show.
3. *Debbie Reynolds,* movie star.
Bride Dolls:
Mona Lisa Series:
Hard plastic dolls with vinyl heads.
1. High heeled fashion dolls.
2. Ballerinas with shoes styled by Capezio.
Dressmaker Dolls with fitting form. Trimmings, basic materials and sleeve board were included.
It is often difficult to identify such dolls because many of them are not marked.

Ballerinas: Valentine made beautiful ballerinas that are fully-jointed including jointed ankles so that the dolls could be dancing *en pointe.* Today their costumes are often bright and beautiful, and a new generation of little girls enjoys the dancing dollies.
SEE: *Illustration 163,* page 71 (Ballerina Section). *Illustration 164,* page 73 (Ballerina Section). *Illustration 165,* page 74 (Ballerina Section).

Lu Ann Simms; (see Roberta and Horsman Companies): HP; 14in (35.6cm); head turning walker; regular walking mechanism with semi-circle cut on leg under body; very long, black hair in pony tail; open mouth with four teeth; felt tongue; arm hook (see Identification Guide, page 266P); 2nd and 3rd fingers molded together; brown eyes; but others have blue eyes; original clothes with *Lu Ann Simms* purse; purple print dress; black velvet trim; white blouse; circa 1953.
MARKS: "Made in USA, Pat. Pend." (back)
SEE: *Illustration 529* (doll). *(Pat Parton Collection.) Illustration 530* (face). *(Pat Parton Collection.)*
PRICE: $55-75

Illustration 529.

VANITY

DOLLS NOT PHOTOGRAPHED BY AUTHORS:

Girl: 23in (58.4cm); HP head; cloth body; latex arms and legs; black mohair wig; open mouth with two teeth; circa 1949.

MARKS: None

VIRGA

In the early 1950s all doll manufacturers were competing to capture the growing U.S. doll market. Two types of dolls had become very popular. One was the 7 to 8in (17.8 to 20.3cm) walking doll modeled after the popular *Ginny* by Vogue. The other was the 6 to 9in (15.2 to 22.9cm) fashion doll which was meant for display rather than play. Both were eagerly collected by both little girls and collectors, and they can be found in many collections today.

Both types of Virga dolls had the same characteristics as those of Fortune and Beehler Arts.

In the Virga line the *Lucy* doll was their *Ginny* look-alike.

CHARACTERISTICS OF VIRGA AND FORTUNE SMALL WALKING DOLLS -- *LUCY* AND *PAM:*

1. Tube-like arm hook (see Identification Guide, page 266O).
2. Molded on T-strap shoes.
3. Molded eyelashes.
4. Sleep eyes.
5. Crease in center of kneecap.
6. Seamline cut through the back part of ear.
7. Many with molded hair under wig.
8. Deep indentation under lower lip (no dimple).
9. 2nd and 3rd fingers molded together.

The Beehler Arts Company also made small fashion dolls with beautiful clothes. These dolls were used as novelty dolls, advertising dolls and tourist dolls. They were sold to other distributors, like Virga, who marketed them under many names.

CHARACTERISTICS OF VIRGA, FORTUNE FASHION DOLLS:

1. Often had painted eyes, especially on the older styles.
2. Unusual side glancing eyes.
3. Heart-shaped mouth that was closed.
4. Eyelashes painted above eye.
5. Mitten hands with dimples below fingers; or fingers molded together with a separate thumb.
6. Plain painted shoes or plain shoes with a molded band (see Identification Guide, page 284E and 284F).
7. Many had net underpants and used much netting in the costumes.
8. Pronounced mold mark directly below wrist line.
9. Single line on seat on many of the dolls.
10. Often missing a navel.
11. Standard arm hook with a slight variation occasionally.
12. Less chubby than the PMA dolls.

Virga competed with dolls made by Plastic Molded Arts. It is interesting for the collector to compare the two main types of these kinds of dolls.

Lucy: HP; 7½in (19.1cm); head turning walker; tube-like arm hook (see Identification Guide, page 265O); 2nd and 3rd fingers molded together; closed mouth; often made as an Indian, Hawaiian, black; molded strap shoe; crease in center of knee cap; seam lines cut through the back part of ear; deep indentation under lower lip but no dimple; brown dress; green trim; circa 1956.

MARKS: None; or "Virga"
SEE: *Illustration 537.*
PRICE: $25-30

Illustration 537.   *Illustration 538.*

Illustration 539.   *Illustration 540.*

Illustration 541.

Schiaparelli (GoGo): vinyl head; HP; 8in (20.3cm); head turning walker; closed mouth; golden blonde hair; Virga body characteristics; clothes designed by noted designer, Schiaparelli, and marketed in a distinctive "shocking pink" box; arm hook (see Identification Guide, page 265K); bridal outfit of white satin and lace; white lace veil; bouquet of white flowers; circa 1956 to 1957.

MARKS: "Virga" (head)
SEE: *Illustration 538.*
PRICE: $85-100 (with trunk and outfits)

UNKNOWN WALKING DOLL WITH VIRGA-FORTUNE CHARACTERISTICS

Girl: HP; 8in (20.3cm); adult body with pointed, mature bust; 1st, 2nd, 3rd fingers molded together; single line seat; high heeled legs; very shiny plastic; jointed knees with long legs below joint; balanced, fluttery eyes; sleep eyes; only lashes painted above eyes; hip pin walker; pin hidden; standard arm hook with a slight variation of a ridge on one side; pink dress with embroidered overskirt which is original; good quality doll which was in competition with Alexander's *Cissette*.

MARKS: None; "11" (left arm); "14" (right arm)
SEE: *Illustration 539* (doll). *(Pat Parton Collection.) Illustration 540* (Virga type compared with *Cissette*). *Illustration 541* (Virga typed compared with *Cissette*-back).
PRICE: $8-12

Unmarked Doll with Virga-Fortune characteristics:

Girl: good quality shiny HP; 10in (25.4cm); head turning walker; jointed at neck, elbows, arms, legs, knees; sleep eyes with molded lashes; vibrant dark, blue eyes with large black pupils that flutter; bright red lips; 1st, 2nd, 3rd fingers molded together; single line on seat; semi-heeled feet; arm hook (see Identification Guide, page 263C); doll is similar to Alexander *Lissy.*

  MARKS: None
  SEE: *Illustration 542* (doll and Alexander *Lissy* on right). *(Louise Schnell Collection.) Illustration 543* (doll and Alexander *Lissy*-back). *(Louise Schnell Collection.)*
  PRICE: $25-30

The following dolls have side glacing painted eyes.   Some are marked. All have Virga-Fortune characteristics. See Virga-Fortune characteristics, page 240.

Mary, Mary, Quite Contrary: HP; 5in (12.7cm); Virga characteristics; yellow dress with the words of the nursery rhyme; white hat; early 1950s.
  MARKS: "Virga" (back); box "Virga Doll" (in script)
  SEE: *Illustration 544.*
  PRICE: $10-15 (in box)

Hawaiian: HP; 7in (17.8cm); Virga characteristics; skirt of varigated fringe-type thread; green satin bra; lei of ribbon-type thread (see Identification Guide, page 284F).
  MARKS: None
  SEE: *Illustration 545.*
  PRICE: $8-10

Illustration 542.

Illustration 543.

Illustration 544.

Illustration 545.

Valentine Girl: HP; 7½in (19.1cm); Virga characteristics; white dress with red felt hearts and lace; hat is a red Valentine; early 1950s.

    MARKS: None

    SEE: *Illustration 546.*

    PRICE: $8-10

Miss Brittany France: HP; Virga characteristics; black top and skirt; underskirt of white, yellow and red satin; lace hat; early 1950s.

    MARKS: None; box has "Virga Doll, Beehler Arts"

    SEE: *Illustration 547* (doll). *(Sophie Zeman Collection.) Illustration 548* (box). *(Sophie Zeman Collection.) Illustration 549* (side of box). *(Sophie Zeman Collection.)*

    PRICE: $10-15 (in box)

Illustration 546.

Illustration 547.

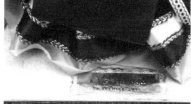

Illustration 548.

Illustration 549.

South American: HP; Virga characteristics; dark rose taffeta skirt; blue ribbon top; black with white polka dot hat and veil; early 1950s.

    MARKS: None; box reads "Virga Doll, Beehler Arts"

    SEE: *Illustration 550. (Sophie Zeman Collection.)*

    PRICE: $10-15 (in box)

Blonde Girl: HP; 5½in (14cm); Virga characteristics; blue printed taffeta dress; lighter blue net overskirt; early 1950s.

    MARKS: "Virga"

    SEE: *Illustration 551. (Marie Ezzo Collection.)*

    PRICE: $8-10

Del Rio: HP; 7½in (19.1cm); Virga characteristics; purple top; yellow ruffled skirt; purple hat with fruit; circa 1950.

    MARKS: None

    SEE: *Illustration 552. (Dolly Jakubecz Collection.)*

    PRICE: $8-10

DOLLS NOT PHOTOGRAPHED

ChiChi: vinyl head; HP; 12½in (31.8cm); high heeled; sleep eyes; molded lashes; circa 1956.

    MARKS: "Doll created by Elsa Schiaparelli" (tag)

Illustration 550.

Illustration 551.

Illustration 552.

VOGUE

The story of Mrs. Jenny Graves, the founder of the Vogue Doll Company, is a moving story and has been told many times. A true pioneer in her field, she created a new genre of dolls that children still love. Even today the 8in (20.3cm) doll is eagerly purchased by parents because of its size and cuteness. Her *Ginny* doll was one of the most widely imitated dolls ever.

Along with Terri Lee Doll Co., Mrs. Graves opened up the doll market to costumes and fashions. Little girls eagerly awaited the new *Ginny* dresses for every important occasion. The clothes were well made and easy for a child to manipulate. Today *Ginny* clothes in excellent condition are hard to find and command high prices.

Many major pattern companies issued patterns for *Ginny*. Today the collector is "discovering" the lovely *Jill* doll. She, too, had a wonderful wardrobe that gives an accurate picture of the clothes of that time.

Ginny-**General Characteristics:**   HP; 8in (20.3cm); fully-jointed knee added later; various types of eyes; 3rd and 4th fingers molded together; arm hook (see Identification Guide, page 267R); feet have good toe detail; mold joint behind ear.
  MARKS: Various
Ginny: HP; 8in (20.3cm); painted eyes; molded hair with mohair wigs; 1948 to 1950.
  MARKS: "Vogue" (head); "Vogue" (body)
  SEE: *Illustration 553 (Alice);* pink nylon top; blue underskirt; white overskirt. *(Ursula Schink and Kathy Zimmerman Collection.) Illustration 554* (girl); yellow nylon dress; pink ribbons. *(Ursula Schink and Kathy Zimmerman Collection.)*
  PRICE: $175-200 plus

Illustration 553.

Illustration 554.

Illustration 555.

Illustration 556.

Illustration 557.

Ginny: HP; 8in (20.3cm); sleep eyes with painted lashes; original clothes; straight legs; left: white taffeta and lace bridal dress with matching veil; right: blue cotton dress trimmed with pink braid; 1950 to 1953.
MARKS: "Vogue" (head); "Vogue" (body)
SEE: *Illustration 555. (Cindy Bezdek Collection.)*
PRICE: $160-185

Ginny: HP; 8in (20.3cm); bubble wool wig; painted lashes above eyes; straight legs; original clothes; black velvet skirt; pink organdy top; straw hat; made for one year only; 1952.
MARKS: "Vogue" (head); "Vogue" (body)
SEE: *Illustration 556.*
PRICE: $250-300

Ginny: HP; 8in (20.3cm); walking doll; still had painted lashes; original clothes; left: white dress with blue and red polka dots, bright red shoes and hat; right: pink nylon dress trimmed in white, blue bow and hat; 1954.
MARKS: "Ginny" (head); "Vogue Dolls, Inc. Pat. #2687594 Made in USA" (body)
SEE: *Illustration 557. (Cindy Bezdek Collection.)*
PRICE: $125-135

Illustration 558.

Illustration 559.

Illustration 560.

Ginny: HP; 8in (20.3cm); plastic molded eyelashes; original clothes; pink snowsuit with gray pants and collar; gray braid on jacket; pink hat; 1955.

> **MARKS:** "Vogue"(head); "Ginny Vogue Dolls, Inc. Pat #2687594 Made in U.S.A."
>
> **SEE:** *Illustration 558* (left doll only).
>
> **PRICE:** $100-125

Ginny: HP; bending knees added and continued for some years; green felt skirt; red blouse; red straw hat; carrying a gun; 1957.

> **MARKS:** "Vogue"(head); "Ginny Vogue Dolls, Inc. Pat #2687594 Made in U.S.A."
>
> **SEE:** *Illustration 559* (cowgirl).
>
> **PRICE:** $100-125

Ginny: HP; bending knees; this was the basic doll that was sold. Clothes and accessories could be purchased and patterns for home sewing were available; 1955.

> **MARKS:** "Vogue" (head); "Ginny Vogue Dolls, Inc. Pat #2687594 Made in U.S.A."
>
> **SEE:** *Illustration 560. (Helen Kirschnick Collection.)*
>
> **PRICE:** $85-95

Illustration 561.

Ginny: vinyl head; HP body; 8in (20.3cm); closed mouth; rooted hair; sleep eyes with lashes; turquoise velveteen coat with pink pompons; pink rabbit skin tam; 1963.

    MARKS: "Ginny" (head); "Ginny, Vogue Dolls, Inc. Pat. No. 2687594 Made in U.S.A." (back)

    SEE: *Illustration 561. (Barbara Comienski Collection.)*

    PRICE: $70-85

Jill: HP; 10in (25.4cm); sleep eyes with molded lashes; pierced ears; jointed knees; high-heeled feet; painted fingernails; adult figure; armhole hook similar to *Ginny;* brochure shows many of the fashions of the period for teen-age girls.

> **MARKS:** "Vogue" (head); "Jill/ Vogue, Made in USA, 1957" (body)
>
> **SEE:** *Illustration 562* (black dress; white hat; pearl necklace; white flower). *Illustration 563* (blue checked wool coat; pink ribbon). *(Louise Schnell Collection.) Illustration 564* (bride; white satin and lace gown). *(Laura Brown Collection.)*
>
> **PRICE:** $65-75 for *Jill* in Vogue clothes

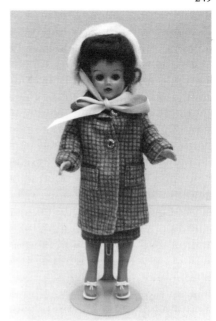

Illustration 563.

Illustration 562.

Illustration 564.

Jill
    Illustration 565. (brochure front cover)
Jill
    Illustration 566. (brochure, page 30)

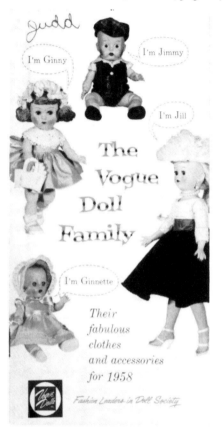

Illustration 565.

I'm a teenager!
Ginny's and
Ginnette's big
sister. I just love to play
grown-up . . . don't you?
I have the most fabulous
collection of high fashion
clothes you have ever seen!
My swim suit is actually
Riviera-inspired . . . and
my sailor dress and
hat are just like those
in the fashion magazines! But wait . . . let's
have fun together and look at all my exciting
new outfits on the following pages.

Jill is 10½ inches tall. She stands, sleeps,
walks, bends her knees and crosses her
ankles. Available with blonde, brunette
or auburn hair in angle cut or ponytail.

Dressed in leotard and high heels — **$3.00**

Illustration 566.

Jill

Illustration 567. (brochure, pages 32 and 33)

Outfit 3300 $1.00†
For Jill's modern dance lessons she wears a jersey leotard. Available in a choice of pink, black or red.

Outfit 3302 $1.00
Here Jill wears her lace edged parchment nylon petticoat and embroidered cotton bra. Her step-ins are nylon tricot.

Outfit 3311 $1.50
And so to bed! — wearing a night-gown of pink nylon that's trimmed with delicate lace and touched at the waist with a flower bud.

Outfit 3312 $1.50†
All heads turn when Jill wears her bright red Capri-pants and match-ing harlequin pattern over-blouse. Her glasses are white plastic.

Outfit 3304 $1.00
For lounging or at bedtime . . . Jill wears her red and white polka dot pajamas with snap buttons and sparkling white rick rack trim.

Outfit 3305 $1.00
Three-quarter length dormitory robe in white cotton with red kerchief design . . . perfect com-panion for Jill's polka dot pajamas.

Outfit 3313 $1.50
Pretty little block print cotton in pale pink with strapless bodice, full skirt, and bands of black ribbon on hem and neckline.

Outfit 3314 $1.50
Dance-ballerina-dance — in layer upon layer of black nylon tulle over a bodice of pink taffeta. At the waist, a festoon of flowers.

† Matching Ginny outfit

† Matching Ginny outfit

Illustration 567.

Illustration 568. (brochure, pages 34 and 35)

Outfit 3315 $1.50
A truly lovely gown for every dress-up occasion. Jacquard taffeta skirt in pale blue, with a jewel trimmed blue velveteen bodice.

Outfit 3316 $1.50
Slim and trim for any occasion ... beige felt sheath skirt topped with a perky brown cotton blouse. At the waist, a brown belt.

Dressed 3131 $5.00 Outfit 3331 $2.90
A slim, kick pleated skirt in fleecy pale pink ... and with it, a red jersey wrap-around blouse sparked with a jewel.

Dressed 3132 $5.00 Outfit 3332 $2.00†
What a beautiful little cotton this is! Every line so new and smart. The blouse is aqua ... the skirt white with aqua flower print.

Outfit 3317 $1.50
Going to a square dance? Jill wears her sparkling gold-tone print skirt with eyelet embroidered blouse and trim black belt.

Dressed 3130 $5.00 Outfit 3330 $2.00†
Such a smart little sundress! This one of white polished cotton banded with black and trimmed with lace on the square neckline.

Dressed 3133 $5.00 Outfit 3333 $2.00†
Jill in blue denim jeans, white cotton shirt and trim little belt. She wears saucy glasses and carries a bottle of "Coke."**

Dressed 3134 $5.00 Outfit 3334 $2.00†
For a summer day, Jill wears a princess dress of primrose yellow cotton. The skirt is full, the neckline and sleeves trimmed with lace.

† Matching Ginny outfit

** "Coca-Cola" and "Coke" are registered trade-marks of the Coca-Cola Company.

Illustration 568.

Jill

Illustration 569. (brochure, pages 36 and 37)

Dressed 3135 $5.00 Outfit 3335 $2.00†
Perfect for every leisure hour . . . striped Ivy League shorts, red jersey shirt and matching knee length socks.

Dressed 3136 $5.00 Outfit 3336 $2.00†
Pretty as a picture, this red and white cotton polka dot dress has a full flaring skirt, black belt, and perky little black bow.

Dressed 3135 $5.00 Outfit 3339 $2.00†
So chic in slim-Jim pants of red, black and white plaid! And the bulky-knit sweater, new as new with big collar and brass buttons.

Dressed 3140 $5.00 Outfit 3340 $2.00
Jill captures the mood of summertime in pink flocked nylon a-flutter with lace trim and lace edged petticoat. In her hair, a butterfly clip.

Dressed 3137 $5.00 Outfit 3337 $2.00†
Beige twill jodhpurs for riding or relaxing . . . and with them a print blouse, bright collar pin and brown boots.

Dressed 3138 $5.00 Outfit 3338 $2.00†
Red and white candy striped cotton . . . gay as can be with swirling skirt, lace trim on the sleeves and sparkling white belt.

Outfit 3345 $2.00
For rainy days, Jill wears this pretty hooded raincoat in assorted prints under clear vinyl. Gay striped bag.

Dressed 3160 $6.00 Outfit 3360 $3.00
Smart little cotton shirtmaker has a black pleated skirt, black belt, white blouse and black and aqua tie. Glasses are black.

† Matching Ginny outfit   † Matching Ginny outfit

Illustration 569.

Jill
Illustration 570. (brochure, pages 38 and 39)

Dressed 3161 $6.00 Outfit 3361 $3.00†
An irresistible little polished cotton fashioned in pale pink with a tiny waist, full skirt and pink jersey shrug.

Dressed 3162 $6.00 Outfit 3362 $3.00
Gay beach days ahead when Jill wears this white princess swim suit, matching cape and red coolie hat. She carries a terry towel.

Dressed 3165 $6.00 Outfit 3365 $3.00
For enchanted hours, Jill wears a lovely gown fashioned with bouffant skirt and dramatic bow. White lace over rustling toast taffeta.

Dressed 3166 $6.00 Outfit 3366 $3.00†
Bright and beautiful! Fireman red sailor dress with white trim, white satin tie . . . and topped with a white felt hat banded in red.

Dressed 3163 $6.00 Outfit 3363 $3.00†
The Record-Hop skirt in swirling yellow felt imprinted in black with gay musical motifs. With it, a blouse of jet black jersey.

Dressed 3164 $6.00 Outfit 3364 $3.00†
Jill's beautiful coral jersey skating dress gleams with silver threads. Her matching hat a-swirl with real feathers. Skates included.

Dressed 3167 $6.00 Outfit 3367 $3.00††
Against the sugary snow . . . black felt ski pants, aqua bloused jacket trimmed with white, black earmuff cap . . . skis and poles.

Dressed 3168 $6.00 Outfit 3368 $3.00
Prints are so new! This one in sheer cotton, in delicate shades of rose. With the dress a pink clutch purse and matching pleated ribbon hat.

† Matching Ginny outfit

†† Matching Ginny and Ginnette outfits

Illustration 570.

Jill

Illustration 571. (brochure, pages 40 and 41)

Dressed 3169 $6.00   Outfit 3369 $3.00
Jill takes all the honors when wearing her plaid pleated skirt, red short sleeve jersey top and white felt blazer with colorful emblem.

Dressed 3170 $6.00   Outfit 3370 $3.00
Beautiful strapless dress in a sari print of brilliant blue nylon. Irridescent taffeta underskirt and lined jacket of silver lamé.

Dressed 3181 $7.00   Outfit 3381 $4.00
Wonderful fleecy two-piece suit in Dior blue has flaring skirt and rhinestone buttoned jacket. She wears a wheat straw hat.

Dressed 3182 $7.00   Outfit 3382 $4.00
Enchantingly beautiful gown of black velveteen and pink lace. Low at the neckline, cinched at the waist. Her hat pure flattery.

Outfit 3175 $3.00
Sophisticated shawl collared coat in beige felt has the very newest lines. Matching cloche sweeps back to show Jill at her prettiest!

Dressed 3180 $7.00   Outfit 3380 $4.00
Graceful, flowing strapless gown in apricot flowered print with lace and moss green velvet trim. For her hair, a flower wreath.

Outfit 3385 $4.00
How beautiful Jill looks in her coat of brilliant red suedine. Round collar and flower trimmed beret of real bunny fur.

Dressed 3190 $8.00   Outfit 3390 $5.00
For after six o'clock, Jill wears a gown of eggshell brocade. Cummerbund, petticoat and satin hat in aqua. Real ranch mink muff.

Illustration 571.

Jill

Illustration 572. (brochure, pages 42 and 43)

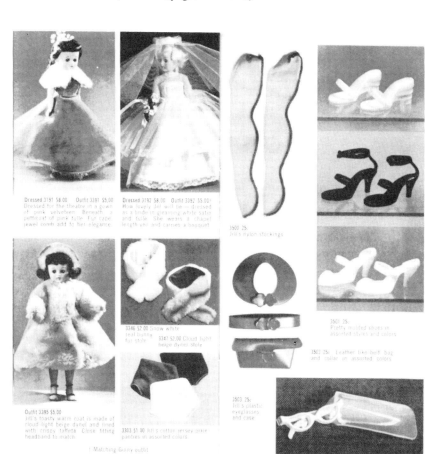

Illustration 572.

Illustration 573.

Illustration 574.

Li'l Imp (*Ginny* Doll Family): HP; vinyl head; 10½in (26.7cm); orange hair; freckles; open/closed mouth; arched eyebrows; jointed knees; dimples on back of hands; head turning walker; sleep eyes; 2nd and 3rd fingers molded together; arm hook (see Identification Guide, page 269Y).

> **MARKS:** Arranbee was purchased by Vogue about 1957. Both *Li'l Imp* and the *Littlest Angel* are the same doll, marked the same way. However, one was put on the market in a Vogue Doll Inc., box. The other was put in an R & B box. Vogue distributed *Li'l Imp* marked R & B. The tag says, "I'm saucy, freckle-faced tomboy, twinkling green eyed pixie; red headed little busybody, Vogue Dolls, Inc."
>
> **SEE:** *Illustration 573.* Left doll: green imp costume with bell on hat; right doll: white satin angel; gold wings; gold rickrack halo. *Illustration 574.* Blue, cotton dress with pink and white embroidery, the extra dress is white with a green print; trimmed with green ribbon.
>
> **PRICE:** $75-90 for *Illustration 573*
> $35-45 for *Illustration 574.*

Vogue marketed an extensive line of clothes for *Li'l Imp.* They came with the outfit and socks and shoes. Shoes have "Fairyland Doll Company" on bottom; clothes tagged "Vogue." *Illustration 574.*

DOLLS NOT PHOTOGRAPHED

Crib Crowd: HP; 8in (20.3cm); baby; legs bent; fully-jointed; painted eyes; sleep eyes with no lashes; 1950.

> **MARKS:** "Vogue" (head)

Wee Imp-Ginny Walker: 8in (20.3cm); red haired and freckled; one year only; 1960.

WALKALON, MFG. CO.

DOLLS NOT PHOTOGRAPHED

Girl: HP; 20-21in (50.8-53.3cm); flat walking foot mechanism; key wind; closed mouth.

> **MARKS:** "Walkalon Mfg. Co."

WILSON

DOLLS NOT PHOTOGRAPHED

Girl: vinyl head; HP; 20in (50.8cm); rooted hair; sleep eyes; walker construction; jointed knees; closed mouth.

> **MARKS:** "W. J. Wilson" (head); "190/Made in USA" (body)

Doll Marks

The following identifying marks are a combination of original research and a checking of the literature in the doll field. It is intended only as a guide and starting point for identifying your doll. The authors found wide variations in the accuracy of marks, especially in the early era of hard plastic dolls.

Many doll companies bought the same bodies and parts from body part firms. Often the marks were used by several different companies that assembled the dolls.

To compound the problem, many of the companies making finished dolls did not mark some hard plastic dolls when they were sold to specific retailers or mail order houses. Often these companies would not admit to manufacturing the dolls if they did not give them the trademark name. In many cases the quality standards of the unmarked doll were very different from that of the marked doll.

An example comes from the Ideal Company. In answer to the authors' question about unmarked dolls, Ms. Joanne Calhoun of the Sales Promotion staff of CBS Toys (Ideal) said, "I have been told by engineers at Ideal with long service in the company that Ideal did make dolls for retailers, but that in these cases they did not identify them as Ideal dolls. That would answer your questions on the Saucy Walker Doll."

NUMBERS

1.	2S	Uneeda
2.	3	Uneeda, Richwood Toys
3.	7/3	Starr
4.	9	Ideal Tiny Tot
5.	11 VW	Valentine
6.	12	Valentine
7.	14	Roberta, Valentine, Star, Desota, Arrow
8.	14R	Eegee
9.	16	Arranbee
10.	16VW	Valentine
11.	P 16	Belle
12.	17VW	Valentine
13.	18VW	Valentine
14.	20	Uneeda
15.	20HH	Belle
16.	VP 23 or UP 17	Ideal
17.	23 ARV	Arranbee
18.	25	Uneeda
19.	31AE	Horsman
20.	32	Ideal
21.	49 R & B	Arranbee
22.	65 R & B	Arranbee
23.	74	Arrow
24.	88	Horsman
25.	V 91	Ideal
26.	P90-91-92-93-94	Ideal

27.	P90 W	Ideal
28.	128	Valentine
29.	160-170-180	Horsman
30.	180	Roberta
31.	R 185	Valentine
32.	190	Wilson
33.	AE 200	Belle
34.	P 200	Ideal
35.	210	Mollye, Arranbee, Uneeda, Roberta
36.	250 R & B	Arranbee
37.	450	Mollye
38.	AE 593	Belle
39.	750	Sayco
40.	2252077	Ideal
41.	2675644	American Character
42.	2687594	Vogue

PAT. PENDING - Companies using this mark
1. A & H (Pats. Pending)
2. Arranbee
3. Ideal Posie (back of knees on roll joint)
4. Ideal
5. Togs & Dolls
6. Terri Lee
7. Valentine (This company sometimes has both "Made in USA" and "Pat. Pending" on back.)

MADE IN U.S.A.
1. Bal
2. Cast
3. Desota
4. Horsman
5. Ideal
6. Imperial
7. Roberta
8. Star
9. Sayco
10. Uneeda
11. Vogue

SYMBOLS
1. ⬦ Arrow
2. Ⓧ Mollye
3. △ Saucy Walker Type - Ideal characteristics

LETTERS - Companies using these letters

1. A   Uneeda
2. A.C.   American Character
3. AE   Belle, Valentine, Sayco
4. Amer.Char.   American Character
5. B   Uneeda
6. Ⓒ   Terri Lee
7. CDC   Cosmopolitan
8. E.G.   Eegee
9. MK   Ideal
10. P   Ideal
11. PMA   Plastic Molded Arts
12. R & B   Arranbee
13. S   Eegee
14. U   Uneeda
15. V   Ideal
16. V4   Effanbee
17. VP   Ideal
18. W   Ideal walker

MARKS USED BY THE ALEXANDER DOLL COMPANY FOR HARD PLASTIC DOLLS

1. Alex.
2. Alexander
3. Mme. Alexander

Identification Guide

TABLE OF CONTENTS

JOINTED ANKLES

The following companies made dolls with jointed ankles:

1. Alexander - *Elise*
2. Belle - Ballerina Doll
3. Eegee - Ballerina Doll
4. Effanbee - *Junior Miss*
5. Horsman - Ballerina
6. Mollye Ballerina
7. Uneeda - *Dollikins*
8. Valentine - Ballerinas

The following companies made dolls with pointed ballerina toes but not jointed ankles:

1. Fortune - *Pam*
2. Valentine - Ballerina

ARM HOOKS

Of all the methods of identifying hard plastic dolls, the characteristics of the arm hooks can be the most helpful. Many of the companies seemed to have their own special hook even though they purchased bodies from the few doll body companies. The following pictures show hooks which have been found on many marked dolls from the same company.

WARNING

The collector must be aware of the so-called "marriages" in repaired dolls. Arms seemed to be especially vulnerable in dolls that were strung, and they were often replaced.

Illustration 575.   *Illustration 576.*

A. Standard arm hook used by many companies - Alexander, Mary Hoyer, Eugenia. These seem to be on many of the earlier, more expensive dolls, both marked and unmarked.
   SEE: *Illustration 575.*

B. Alexander *Lissy* hook. Most collectors surveyed were surprised to find their *Lissy* dolls unmarked. This picture will help you identify your doll quickly.
   SEE: *Illustration 576.*

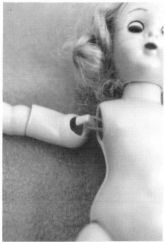

Illustration 577.   *Illustration 578.*

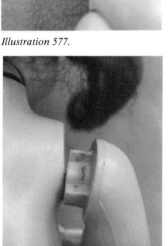

Illustration 579.   *Illustration 580.*

C. Unknown *Lissy* look-alike.
    SEE: *Illustration 577.*

D. Eegee walking hook - *Susan Stroller, Merry Stroller* and others.
    SEE: *Illustration 578.*

E. Standard walking doll hook - Imperial and many more. The hook was built to stop the arm from swinging too high. This helped control the head action.
    SEE: *Illustration 579.*

F. Nancy Ann *Muffie.* Most *Muffies* have markings. However, others do not. Unmarked dolls were sometimes marketed as *Lori Anns.* The Richwood *Sandra Sue* has a similar arm hook.
    SEE: *Illustration 580.*

Illustration 581.

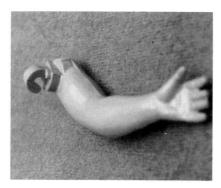

Illustration 582.

Illustration 583.

G. Nancy Ann unmarked *Lori* dolls. These dolls have the same hooks as *Muffie*.
    SEE: *Illustration 581.*

H. Standard Plastic Molded Arts (PMA) small fashion doll. These are found on
    both marked and unmarked dolls. This company supplied bodies for many other
    companies.
    SEE: *Illustration 582.*

I. Variation of Standard Molded Arts small fashion doll hook. This is found on both
    marked and unmarked dolls.
    SEE: *Illustration 583.*

Illustration 584.

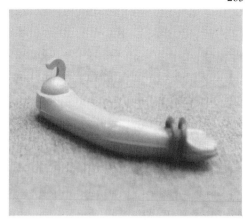

Illustration 585.

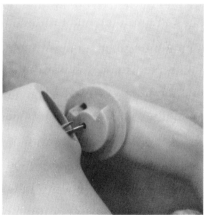

Illustration 586.

Illustration 587.

J. Roberta, Doll Bodies, Inc. prong arm. These hooks have been seen on both marked and unmarked dolls. Often the larger dolls have "Made in USA" in a circle on the back. They were often inexpensive dolls although sometimes the quality is excellent.
   SEE: *Illustration 584.*

K. Standard Virga, Fortune, Beehler Arts, Ontario Plastics very small fashion doll hook and arm. This hook was on the marked Virga Hawaiian doll.
   SEE: *Illustration 585.*

L. Ideal hook seen on vinyl head walking dolls such as *Ruth, Posie* and others. The *Saucy Walkers* of an earlier vintage have a standard walking hook.
   SEE: *Illustration 586.*

M. Plastic Molded Arts (PMA) arm hook on larger doll which competed with *Toni,* Alexander, R & B and others.
   SEE: *Illustration 587.*

Illustration 588.

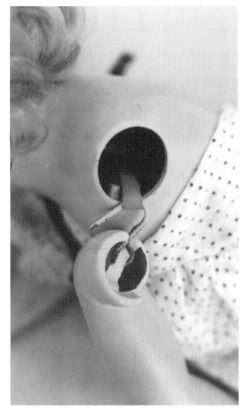

Illustration 590.

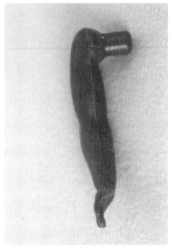

Illustration 589.

N. Cosmopolitan *Ginger* arm hook. The unusual hook has a straight edge and is an excellent identification guide for this unmarked doll. It also is important when an arm is missing and needs replacement.
    SEE: *Illustration 588.*

O. Fortune *Pam* and Virga *Lucy* hook. The hook is tubular and is used on the different sizes of these dolls. The *Ginny* look-alikes are difficult to identify and arm hook identification is helpful.
    SEE: *Illustration 589.*

P. Plastic bar across top of inner arm holds the hook. This is a very common type hook seen on Horsman, Ideal walking dolls, Valentine (VW) dolls.
    SEE: *Illustration 590.*

Illustration 591.

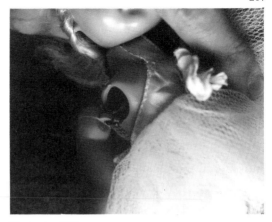

Illustration 592.

Illustration 593.

Illustration 594.

Q.   Horsman, Imperial Crown (IMPCO) variation of standard arm hook. This has a rougher, larger cutout U on the round arm hole.
SEE: *Illustration 591.*

R.   Vogue *Ginny* arm hook. This hook is similar to the Nancy Ann *Muffie* hook. However, the metal piece is more circular while the Nancy Ann *Muffie* and *Lori* hook is more oval.
SEE: *Illustration 592.*

S.   Unusual arm hook on Violetta doll (see page 103). This doll has no markings but has characteristics of a Fortune doll.
SEE: *Illustration 593.*

T.   Togs and Dolls arm hook. This is found in the smaller and larger versions. There is a small plastic prong on the crossbar.
SEE: *Illustration 594.*

Illustration 595.

Illustration 596.

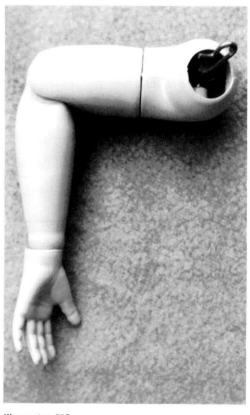

Illustration 597.

U.   Nancy Ann *Debbie* arm hook. This is an important identification feature for this chubby-type doll because the body marking wears off easily.
   SEE: *Illustration 595.*

V.   Duchess arm hook. Most of the time the Duchess doll is well marked. However, some unmarked Duchess dolls have been seen.
   SEE: *Illustration 596.*

W.   Arm and arm hook of Uneeda *Dollikins.* This is one of the most unusual arms of any hard plastic doll.
   SEE: *Illustration 597.*

Illustration 598.

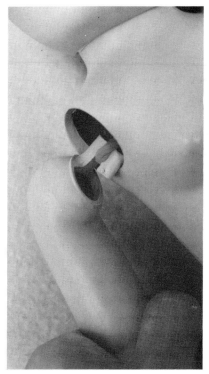

Illustration 599.

X. *Lingerie Lou* by Doll Bodies arm hook. This hook has been seen on both dressed and undressed models. The undressed ones were sold for home sewing. Some dolls have markings. Some do not.
    SEE: *Illustration 598.*

Y. Arranbee *Littlest Angel* and Vogue *Li'l Imp.*
    SEE: *Illustration 599.*

Z. American Character *Sweet Sue.* The lovely *Sweet Sue* walking doll has a very strong spring arm which can differentiate it from other <u>walking</u> dolls with similar faces. If the arm resists pulling, this is probably the reason. Use caution when examining this doll. When repairing this doll, most restorers use a standard string arrangement. The authors have not seen this spring on the non-walking dolls.

BABIES

HP Head, Latex Body

1. Arranbee: *Baby Donna*
2. Eegee: baby
3. Eegee: *Baby Christine*
4. Imperial: *Baby Perry*
5. Ideal: *Baby Gurglee*

HP head, Cloth Body, Composition Arms and Legs

1. Arranbee: *Happy Time*
2. Cosmopolitan: *Baby Emily*
3. Ideal: "Coos Series"
4. Uneeda: *Needa Toddles*

Total Hard Plastic

1. Alexander: *Precious Toddler, Lovey Dovey*
2. American Character: *Baby Lou*
3. Eegee: boy and girl
4. Hollywood: baby
5. Ideal: *Baby Jo*
6. Irwin: baby
7. Rosebud: baby
8. Terri Lee: *Connie Lynn*
9. Vogue: "Crib Crowd"

HP Head, Vinyl Body

1. American Character: *Ricky, Jr.*
2. American Character: *Tiny Tears*
3. Arranbee: *Little Angel Baby*
4. Uneeda: *Baby Dollikins*
5. Alexander: *Little Genius*

HP Head, Cloth Body, Latex Arms and Legs

1. American Character: *Baby Sue*
2. Arranbee: *Baby Donna*
3. Cosmopolitan: *Gloria*
4. Desota: *Heartbeat Baby*
5. Ideal: *Tickletoes*
6. Mollye: *Joanne*
7. Sayco: *Playgirl*
8. Vanity: girl

HP Head, Rubber or Magic Skin

1. American Character: *Tiny Tears, I Love Lucy*
2. Effanbee: *Mommy's Baby, Dy-Dee Baby*
3. Horsman: *Mama Doll*
4. Ideal: *Baby Coos, Sparkle Plenty, Magic Squeeze, Honeysuckle*
5. Imperial: *Linda*

HP Head, Cloth Body, Vinyl Arms and Legs

1. Arranbee: *Little Angel*
Cosmopolitan: *Pam Baby*
3. Ideal: *Baby Plassie, Talking Tot*
4. Imperial: baby
5. Mollye: *Precious Baby*
6. Uneeda: *Needa Toddles*

Pierced Nostrils

1. American Character: *Tiny Tears, I Love Lucy*
2. Ideal: *Baby Jo*
3. Imperial: baby

HP Sticky Heads and Limbs, Cloth Body

1. American Character: *Baby Sue*

HP Shoulder Plate

1. Cosmopolitan: *Gloria, Emily*
2. Effanbee: *Mommy's Baby, Noma, the Electronic Doll*

HP Head, Arms, Legs Cloth Body

1. Ideal: *Plassie*

Crossed Baby Legs

1. American Character: *Miss Chicadee*

CHUBBY TYPE DOLLS

There were many 10in (25.4cm) to 12½in (31.8cm) chubby-type dolls in the 1950s. The early ones were hard plastic but when mothers discovered the joys of rooted hair, doll manufacturers quickly converted to vinyl heads.

1.	Arranbee: *Littlest Angel*	10½in (26.7cm)
2.	Eegee: *Chubby Schoolgirl*	10½in (26.7cm)
3.	Eegee: *Tina* and *Skater*	11in (27.9cm)
4.	Nancy Ann: all-HP *Debbie*	11in (27.9cm)
5.	Nancy Ann: vinyl head *Debbie*	11in (27.9cm)
6.	Pedigree: toddler	
	often found in black versions	10½in (26.7cm)
		12in (30.5cm)
7.	Plastic Molded Arts: *Petite Marie*	10in (25.4cm)
8.	Roddy: girls and boys	12in (30.5cm)
		12½in (31.8cm)
9.	Terri Lee: *Tiny Terri* and *Jerri*	10in (25.4cm)
10.	Togs and Dolls	10in (25.4cm)
		12in (30.5cm)
11.	Vogue: *Li'l Imp*	10½in (26.7cm)

DOLLS THAT HAVE MODELS IN BOTH HARD PLASTIC AND VINYL HEADS

1. Alexander: *Elise*
2. A & H: *Gigi*
3. Arranbee: *Nanette*
4. Cosmopolitan: *Ginger*
5. Effanbee: *Honey Walker*
6. Fortune: *Pam*
7. Ideal: *Saucy Walker, Saucy Walker Toddler*
8. Ideal Toni Family
   HP: *Toni, Mary Hartline, Miss Curity,* unmarked dolls
   Vinyl heads: *Harriet Hubbard Ayer, Ruth, Princess Mary, Betsy McCall*
9. Imperial: Girls
10. Nancy Ann: *Muffie* in HP, *Lori Ann* with vinyl head
11. Uneeda: *Needa Toddles* (HP), *Toddles* (vinyl head)
12. Valentine
    HP: *Lu Ann Simms, Roxanne, Debbie Reynolds*
    Vinyl heads: Ballerinas, Girls
13. Virga: *Lucy*
14. Vogue: *Ginny*

EYES

Eyes can be an important identification feature. Unique eyes, lashes and eyebrows may be the only unusual characteristic on some of the early hard plastic dolls.

Not all the dolls of each of the companies listed will have the particular eye characteristic. For further information, turn to the company listing.

MOLDED LASHES
1. American Character: *Betsy McCall*
2. Arranbee: *Littlest Angel*
3. A & H
4. Corrine: bride dolls
5. Cosmopolitan: *Ginger*
6. Doll Bodies: walking dolls
7. Eegee: *Tina*
8. Fortune: *Pam*, Blue Ribbon Classics
9. Hollywood
10. Ideal: *Lindy*, tiny girl
11. Midwestern Mfg. Co.
12. Nancy Ann: late Storybook Dolls, late *Muffie* dolls, *Lori Ann* dolls
13. Plastic Molded Arts: some dolls
14. Pedigree-England
15. Richwood
16. Roberta: small walking dolls
17. Uneeda: *Janie*
18. Valentine: small fashion doll, 19in (48.3cm) high heel doll
19. Virga: *Lucy, Schiaparelli* doll, *Fashion Doll*
20. Vogue: *Ginny, Jill, Li'l Imp*

FEATHERED EYEBROWS
1. Artisan Novelty
2. Alexander
3. Effanbee
4. Eugenia
5. Eegee
6. Ideal
7. Plastic Molded Arts

FLIRTY EYES
1. Freydberg, Inc.: *Mary Jane*
2. Ideal: *Saucy Walker* in HP and vinyl head
3. Uneeda: *Country Girl*

PURPLE EYES
1. Palitoy-England: 7½in (19.1cm) girl

PAINTED EYES 10in (25.4cm) AND UNDER

1. A & H
2. Active
3. American Character
4. Bal
5. Beehler Arts
6. Doll Bodies
7. Duchess
8. El
9. Fairyland
10. Hollywood
11. Irwin
12. Nancy Ann
13. Playhouse
14. S & E
15. Virga
16. Vogue

SLEEP EYES - NO LASHES

1. A & H
2. Desota
3. Doll Bodies
4. Duchess
5. Peggy Huffman
6. Lovely
7. Nancy Ann
8. Plastic Molded Arts
9. Playhouse
10. Rosalie
11. Virga

EYELASH LINES ON SIDE OF EYE

1. Eugenia - 5 lines
2. Freydberg - 4 lines
3. Ideal: *Toni, Harriet Hubbard Ayer* - 3 lines
4. Ottolini - 5 lines
5. Uneeda: *Janie* - 3 lines
6. Valentine: small fashion doll - 3 lines

FACES

FLAT VINYL FACES

1. Belle
2. Mollye
3. Uneeda
4. Valentine

POINTED CHINS

1. Arranbee
2. Mary Hoyer
3. Roberta

PAINTED EYES 11in (27.9cm) AND UP

1. Bed dolls
2. Freydberg
3. H. D. Lee
4. Ideal
5. Latexture
6. Terri Lee

FLUTTERY EYES

1. Alexander
2. Fortune
3. Furga
4. Peggy Huffman
5. Lovely
6. Roddy
7. Virga

EYESHADOW

1. American Character: some *Sweet Sues*
2. Artisan Novelty
3. Cosmopolitan: *Baby Pam*
4. Horsman: *Baby Betty Ann*
5. Hoyer, Mary
6. Ideal: *Mary Hartline, Miss Curity*
7. Imperial: baby and girl dolls
8. Ottolini
9. Palitoy: *Scotch Girl*

FINGERS

Individual Fingers

1. Advance: *Winnie* and *Wanda*
2. American Character: *Sweet Sue, Baby Sue, Tiny Tears*
3. Cosmopolitan: *Ginger*
4. Doll Bodies: *Ginny* look-alike
5. Eegee: *Susan Stroller, Miss Debutante, Baby Christine*
6. Effanbee: *Honey, Melodie, Mommy's Baby,* Noma
7. Horsman: most dolls
8. Ideal: *Saucy Walker* types, *Posie* types, *Toni* types
9. Imperial: most dolls
10. Little Nurse
11. Made in U.S.A.
12. Midwestern Dolls
13. Mollye: *Lone Ranger, Tonto, Baby Precious*
14. Nancy Ann: *Muffie, Lori Ann*
15. Roberta: walker
16. Roddy: girls & boys
17. Sayco: girls
18. Togs & Dolls
19. Uneeda: girl
20. Valentine Ballerinas and high heeled girls

2nd and 3rd Fingers Molded Together

1. A & H: many dolls
2. American Character: *Sweet Sue*
3. Arranbee: *Nannette, Nancy*
4. Artisan Novelty: *Miss Gadabout, Raving Beauty*
5. Corrine
6. Eugenia: girl
7. Fortune: *Pam*
8. Freydberg: *Mary Jane*
9. Lovely Doll
10. Mollye: *Dancing Deb* and others
11. Nancy Ann: *Style Show*
12. PMA: most dolls
13. Roberta: many
14. Uneeda: *Dollikins, Janie*
15. Virga: *Lucy*

1st, 2nd, 3rd, 4th Fingers Molded Together

1. Active Dolls
2. CIPSA
3. Duchess
4. EL
5. Horsman: *Gretel*
6. Hollywood
7. Palitoy
8. Rosalie
9. S & E
10. Virga

1st, 2nd, 3rd Fingers Molded Together

1. Arranbee: *Nannette, Nancy*
2. Fortune Type: *Lissy* look-alike
3. Ottolina-Italy
4. Palitoy-England
5. Richwood Toys
6. Terri Lee: *Tiny Terri*
7. Virga Type

Gauntlet Hands-Palm Down, Open Hands and Fingers Wide Spread

1. Bal
2. Eegee: *Little Susan*
3. Irwin
4. Knickerbocker

FINGERS 1, 2, 3, 4 Molded Together at Bottom, but Separate Near Top

1. A & H: some dolls
2. Corrine: bride dolls
3. Peggy Hoffman

Painted Fingernails

1. Eugenia
2. Furga
3. Uneeda: *Dollikins*
4. Valentine: some ballerinas
5. Vogue: *Jill*

Unusual Characteristics of Fingers

1. Furga: girl in short dress - delicate pointed fingers
2. Ideal: *Harriet Hubbard Ayer* - very long fingers and nails
3. Valentine: some dolls - unusually long slim fingers

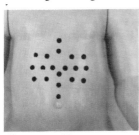

Illustration 600.

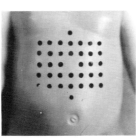

Illustration 601.

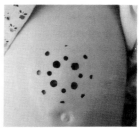

Illustration 602.

GRILLS OR GRID

The *Saucy Walker*-type dolls usually had a grill for a cryer voice. A few other hard plastic dolls had them, also. The authors found this to be an easy method of identification. However, it was not as accurate as some of the other methods.

A. Eegee: 13in (33cm) *Merry Stroller*; vinyl head; HP
   MARKS: "Eegee" (head)
   SEE: *Illustration 600. (Mary Beth Manchook Collection.)*

B. Eegee: 17in (43.2cm) *Susan Stroller*; vinyl head HP
   MARKS: "Eegee" (head)
   SEE: *Illustration 601.*

C. Horsman: 23in (58.4cm) *Saucy Walker* look-alike
   MARKS: none
   SEE: *Illustration 602. (Pat Parton Collection.)*

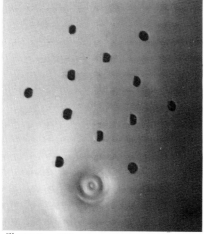

Illustration 603.

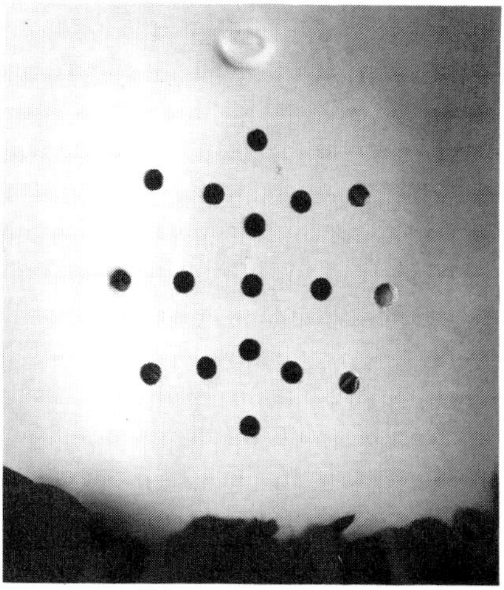

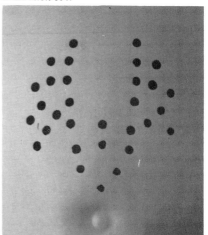

Illustration 604.

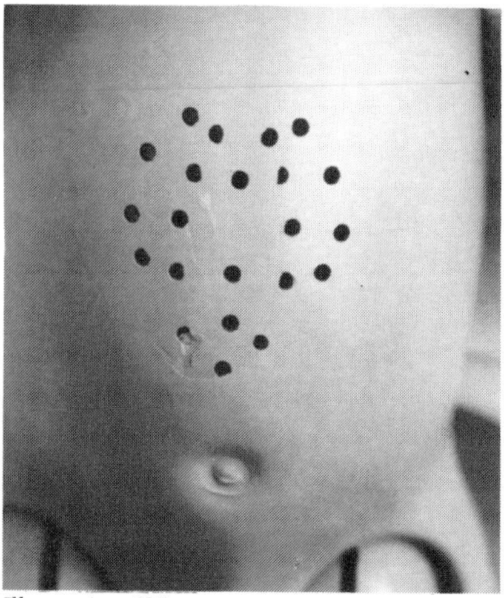

Illustration 605.

Illustration 606.

D.   Ideal: 22in (55.9cm) HP *Saucy Walker*; straight legs.
   MARKS: "Ideal" (head)
   SEE: *Illustration 603.*

E.   Ideal: 23in (58.4cm) vinyl head; HP *Saucy Walker*; straight legs.
   MARKS: "Ideal Doll VP 23" (head)
   SEE: *Illustration 604.*

F.   Ideal Type: 22in (55.9cm) *Saucy Walker* look-alike; HP; straight legs.
   MARKS: △   (head)
   SEE: *Illustration 605.*

G.   Ideal Type: 22in (55.9cm) *Saucy Walker* look-alike; HP; straight legs.
   MARKS: △   (head)
   SEE: *Illustration 606. (Pat Parton Collection.)*

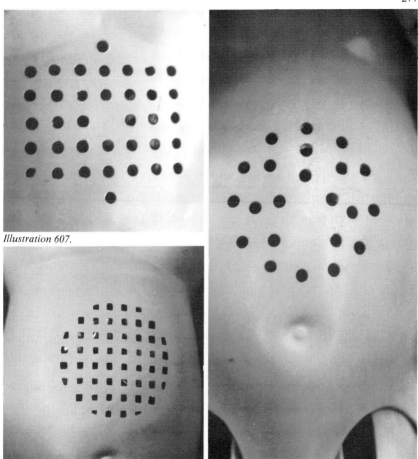

Illustration 607.

Illustration 608.

Illustration 609.

H.   Ideal: 23in (58.4cm) vinyl head; HP; *Posie;* jointed at knees.
MARKS: "Ideal Doll" (head), "Ideal Doll" (body), "Pat. Pending" (back of upper leg)
SEE: *Illustration 607. (Pat Parton Collection.)*

I.   Ideal: 14in (35.6cm) and 16in (40.6cm) *Saucy Walker Toddler* - HP; straight legs.
MARKS: "W" (head); "Ideal Doll W 16" (body) *Saucy Walker Toddler* - vinyl head; HP; straight legs.
"Ideal Doll VP17" (head); "Ideal Doll W16" (body) *Posie Toddler* - vinyl head; HP: jointed at knees.
"Ideal Doll VP 17" (head); "Ideal Doll W16" (body)
SEE: *Illustration 608.*

J.   Imperial: 18in (45.7cm) walker; HP.
MARKS: "Impco" (head)
SEE: *Illustration 609.*

HIGH HEELED DOLLS

Most of the hard plastic dolls had flat feet. Only the later dolls, such as those with vinyl heads had high heels. The transitional rigid vinyl *Revlon, Jan* and many others came in the last years of the 1950s. They changed the entire doll manufacturing business. *Barbie* followed and the whole new "World of Barbie" changed the playing habits of the following generations.

1. Alexander: *Cissy, Cissette, Lissy*
2. Doll Bodies: *Lingerie Lou*
3. Effanbee: *Champagne Lady, Mother, Junior Miss*
4. Foreign (Ottolini): ladies
5. Richwood: *Sandra Sue*
6. Uneeda: *Dollikins*
7. Unknown: PMA characteristics (see page 210, 234)
8. Unknown: Uneeda characteristics (see page 232)
9. Valentine: *Debbie Reynolds*
10. Virga: 12in (30.5cm) Schiaparelli *Chi Chi* (vinyl head)
11. Vogue: *Jill*

KEY WIND

1. Advance: *Wanda* and *Winnie Walker*
2. Irwin: *Spanish Dancer*
3. Mar: walking doll
4. Walkalon Mfg. Co.: girl

KNEES

JOINTED KNEES

The following companies produced some jointed knee dolls. The same companies also produced dolls with straight legs.

1. A & H: *Gigi*
2. American Character: *Betsy McCall, Sweet Sue*
3. Arranbee: *Littlest Angel*
4. Alexander: *Cissette, Lissy, Elise, Cissy*
5. Beehler Arts: *ChiChi*
6. Belle: *Ballerina Belle, Perfect Companion, Twisting Pixie*
7. Cosmopolitan: *Ginger* (some)
8. Eegee: ballerina, *Susan Stroller, Little Debutante, Tina*
9. Effanbee: *Honey Ballerina, Melodie, Mother, Champagne Lady, Junior Miss*
10. Ideal: *Posie, Posie Toddler*, walking girl
11. Made in U.S.A.: girl
12. Mollye: ballerina
13. Nancy Ann: *Debbie*, 10in (25.4cm) *Lori Ann*
14. Valentine: ballerina
15. Vogue: *Ginny, Li'l Imp*
16. Wilson: girl

MOUTHS

In any identification study of hard plastic dolls, a surprising feature quickly emerges. There are very few open mouth dolls. An open mouth with teeth was a popular, sales feature on composition and bisque dolls. However, most dolls of the hard plastic era had closed mouths.

Some companies such as Horsman made many dolls with open mouths and teeth. Others such as Arranbee made only one or two. There were very few dolls with open mouths when the companies turned to vinyl heads and rooted hair.

Another identifying feature is the number of teeth. However, for this guide only the number of exposed teeth will be counted. Companies like Valentine had up to six teeth with one or more inside the head.

Caution must be used in using teeth for identification. Children knocked out teeth which were replaced at the local doll hospital.

COMPANIES WITH OPEN MOUTH DOLLS

1. Advance Doll & Toy Company.
2. Arranbee: *Judy*
3. Artisan Novelty: *Miss Gadabout, Raving Beauty*
4. Belle: Playmate Walker
5. Cosmopolitan: *Pam Baby*
6. Effanbee: *Noma, the Electronic Doll, Mommy's Baby*
7. Eegee: *Baby Christine, Gigi Pereaux*
8. Horsman: child and girl types
9. Ideal: *Saucy Walker, Saucy Toddler, Plassie, Bonnie Braids*
10. Imperial: walking and non-walking girls, babies
11. Made in U.S.A.: girls
12. Mollye: *Margaret Rose, Peggy Rose,* basic doll, walking doll
13. Natural: bride
14. Paris Doll
15. Ravon: girl
16. Roberta: *Lu Ann Simms* and others
17. Roddy: boys and girls
18. Star: *Dorothy Collins*
19. Uneeda: *Needa Toddles*
20. Valentine: *Debbie Reynolds, Lu Ann Simms, Roxanne* and others
21. Vanity: girl

Babies Open/Closed Mouths

1. Eegee: *Baby Christine*
2. Effanbee: *Mommy's Baby*
3. Ideal: *Baby Plassie Tickletoes*
4. Imperial: *Baby Perry*
5. Mollye: *Baby Joan*
6. Terri Lee: *Connie Lynn*

Open Mouth 4 Teeth

1. Arranbee: *Judy*
2. Artisan Novelty: *Little Miss Gad about, Raving Beauty*
3. Belle: *Playmate Walker*
4. Horsman: many dolls
5. Imperial: girl
6. Made in U.S.A.: girl
7. Mollye: basic doll
8. Natural: bride
9. Ravon: girl
10. Roberta: *Lu Ann Simms* and others
11. Valentine: *Lu Ann Simms, Haleloke, Roxanne* and others

Painted Teeth

1. Eegee: *Gigi Pereaux*
2. Ideal: *Bonnie Braids* (3 painted teeth with open/closed mouth)

Baby-Open Mouth Nurser

1. American Character: *Tiny Tears*
2. Effanbee: *Dy-Dee Baby*
3. Imperial: baby
4. Irwin: baby
5. Uneeda: *Baby Dollikins*

Open Mouth 2 Teeth

1. Cosmopolitan: *Baby Emily, Pam*
2. Effanbee: *Mommy's Baby, Noma*
3. Horsman: *Betty Ann*
4. Ideal: *Saucy Walker Saucy Toddler, Plassie, Tickletoes*
5. Mollye: *Baby Joan*
6. Roddy: boys, girls, *Saucy*-type walkers
7. Sayco: baby
8. Uneeda: *Needa Toddles*
9. Vanity: girl

Open/Closed Mouth with Teeth

1. Eegee: *Gigi Pereaux*
2. Rosebud: *Paulie*

Open/Closed Mouth Molded Tongue

1. Alexander: *Madelaine*
2. Arranbee: *Littlest Angel*
3. Eegee: *Susan Stroller*
4. Mollye: vinyl headed dolls
5. Uneeda: *Needa Toddles, Country Girl*
6. Valentine: *Margie*
7. Vogue: *Li'l Imp*

Open Mouth 5 or 6 Teeth

1. Imperial: walking doll
2. Made in U.S.A.
3. Valentine: *Debbie Reynolds* and others

SAUCY WALKER TYPES

Saucy Walker and *Saucy Toddler* were very popular, well-made dolls in both girl and boy models. They were also inexpensive. Other companies, and possibly Ideal itself made cheaper versions which sold well. Some were marked with the competing company name, but many were unmarked or with symbols like △ or AE. They were made of all-hard plastic or a combination of hard plastic body and vinyl head.

CHARACTERISTICS OF SAUCY WALKER TYPE

1. Head turning, pin jointed walker
2. A cryer grill in the stomach
3. Individual fingers
4. Chubby child or toddler body

The following companies competed with Ideal and made a *Saucy Walker* type. See company listings for details.

1. Aster Co.
2. Belle: *Playmate Walker*
3. Eegee: *Susan Stroller* and *Merry Stroller*
4. Horsman: *Ruthie Walker*
5. Imperial: walking girl
6. Pedigree of London: walking boy and girl
7. Roddy of England: boys and girls
8. Uneeda: *Country Girl*

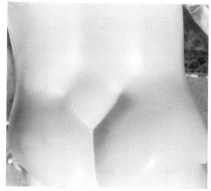

Illustration 610.

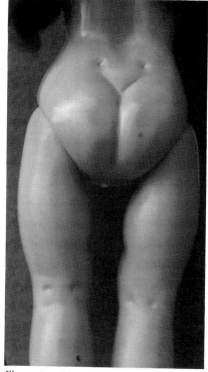

Illustration 611.

SEAT PATTERNS ON DOLLS

A.

B.

C.

1. Ideal *Saucy Walker* types
2. Imperial pin joint walkers
3. Sayco pin joint walkers
4. Uneeda pin joint walkers
5. Unmarked pin joint walkers

SEE: *Illustration 610.*

1. Artisan Novelty
2. Horsman non-walker
3. Ideal *Toni* line
4. Imperial non-walker
5. Richwood *Sandra Sue*
6. Uneeda - a few
7. Valentine (Horsman type heads)

SEE: *Illustration 611.*

1. Fortune, Blue Ribbon, *Violetta, Cissette* and *Lissy* look-alikes, NOT *Pam,* many, many more
2. Nancy Ann *Muffie, Lori Ann*
3. Virga, many, many *Fashion Dolls* NOT *Lucy*

SHOES

Shoes play a part in identifying the hard plastic doll. This section is divided into the following parts:
1. Guide to dolls that have molded or painted shoes
2. Shoes used by specific companies which help to identify their dolls
3. Unusual footwear

SECTION I

There were only a few major companies or groups of companies who actually molded the hard plastic dolls. Other doll firms bought from these major manufacturers and dressed them, or marketed them, or did both. Often the type of shoe mold will offer excellent clues to the identity of the doll.

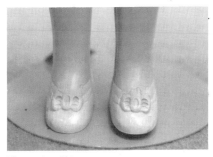

Illustration 612.

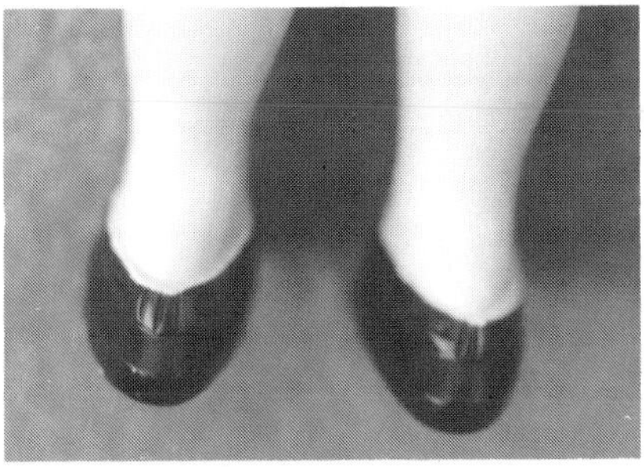

Illustration 613.

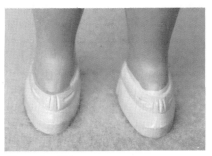

Illustration 614.

Illustration 615.

PLASTIC MOLDED ARTS - Shoes from marked dolls or from dolls in original boxes

A. Molded, painted shoe with bow from 7½in (19.1cm) to 12in (30.5cm) dolls. Along with PMA, A & H, Midwestern and Corrine dolls used this same mold. There are also other companies who used the shoe mold.
   SEE: *Illustration 612.*

B. PMA also made a type of molded, painted shoe with straight lines simulating bows. In addition to PMA, Peggy Huffman, Playhouse and others used this shoe. The two illustrations show white and black shoes.
   SEE: *Illustration 613. Illustration 614.*

C. This unusual mold is on a PMA Indian.
   SEE: *Illustration 615. (Phyllis Appell Collection.)*

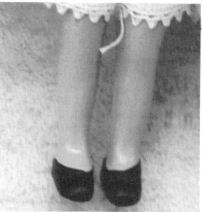

Illustration 617.

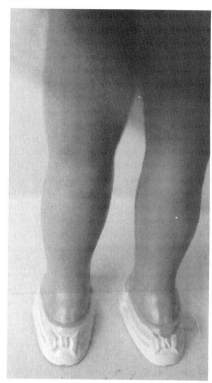

Illustration 616.

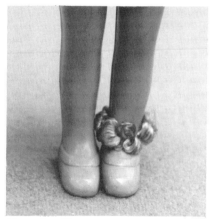

Illustration 618.

MOLDED SHOE FROM OTHER COMPANIES - Dolls have PMA characteristics

D. Molded, painted shoe with bow from 7½in (19.1cm). The bottom of the original plastic see-through box with A & H marking can be seen in the illustration. Other companies with the same shoe are Duchess and *Lingerie Lou* (Doll Bodies). **SEE:** *Illustration 616.*

VIRGA-FORTUNE-BEEHLER ARTS-ONTARIO PLASTICS - Shoes from marked dolls or from dolls in original boxes. All of these shoes are plain and have an upper or bottom roll around the shoe.

E. Virga (Beehler Arts) shoe. This is also seen on Fairyland Dolls
    SEE: *Illustration 617. (Sophie Zeman Collection.)*

F. This is another typical Virga (Beehler Arts) shoe on a Hawaiian tourist doll. It is a very common mold.
    SEE: *Illustration 618.*

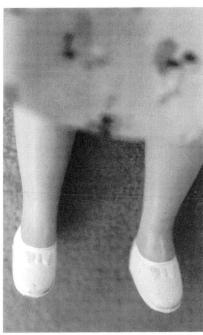

Illustration 619.

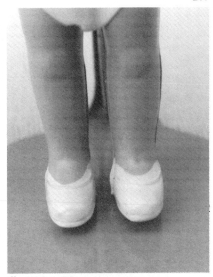

Illustration 620.

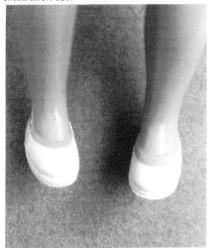

Illustration 621.

G. A Fortune shoe has an upper roll and plain butterfly bow.
    SEE: *Illustration 619.*

H. Fortune also had a simple shoe like Virga with a thinner, upper roll. Other dolls
    with this mold are Rosalie, Active, Marcie (A & H) Duchess.
    SEE: *Illustration 620.*

I. A roll on the bottom of the shoe can be seen on some dolls with Virga-Fortune
    characteristics. This shoe was on a fashion doll with the label Violetta from the
    Opera "La Traviata" by Verdi on her tag.
    SEE: *Illustration 621.*

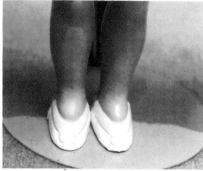

Illustration 622.

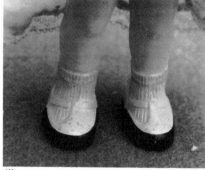

Illustration 624.

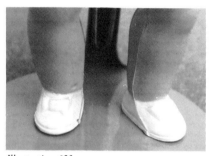

Illustration 623.

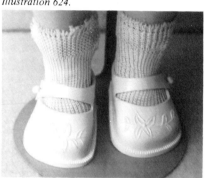

Illustration 625.

LOVELY DOLL COMPANY

J.   This ubiquitous shoe has been found on dolls from the Lovely Doll Company and dolls marked "EL." Some dolls were purchased from a toy wholesaler in Cleveland, Ohio, by the author in 1956 or 1957 and dressed for a charity bazaar. The various dolls with this shoe are very different from each other, and they have both Virga-Fortune and PMA characteristics. For convenience they have been listed under *Lovely Dolls*.
SEE: *Illustration 622.*

ROBERTA

K.   This is a molded, painted simple shoe with bow. The doll was a non-walker that competed with *Ginny*.
SEE: *Illustration 623. (Pat Parton Collection.)*

KNICKERBOCKER, S & E, RELIABLE OF CANADA

L.   These large molded, painted shoes and socks were on tiny 5in (12.7cm) or 6in (15.2cm) dolls.
SEE: *Illustration 624. (Pat Parton Collection.)*

SECTION II - Shoes from Specific Companies

M.   Some Ideal plastic shoes were very pretty. This one had flowers on the toes. Other Ideal shoes were molded the same but without the flowers. They were marked "Ideal" on the bottom of the shoe.
SEE: *Illustration 625.*

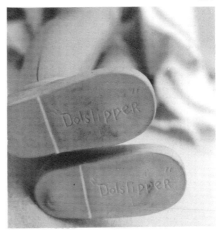

Illustration 627.

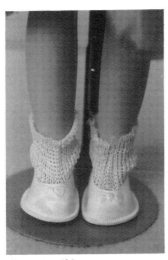

Illustration 626.

Illustration 628.

N. Design shoes used by A & H
   SEE: *Illustration 626.*

O. These shoes were found on the Ideal *Princess Mary* twins. They are probably original, but if they are not, they are of the 1950s period. They are distinctive and are blue.
   SEE: *Illustration 627. (Pat Parton Collection.)*

SECTION III. Unusual Shoes

CAPEZIO

P. These lovely plastic ballet slippers were on a Valentine Doll. The company advertised that their ballet slippers were designed by the well-known ballet shoemaker.
   MARKS: Capezio Since 1887
   Dancers Cobbler
   SEE: *Illustration 628.*

UNUSUAL IDENTIFICATION FEATURES

Ears
1. Effanbee: *Dy-Dee Baby,* applied rubber ears

Musical Dolls
1. A & H: *Musical Sweetheart*
2. Ideal: *Musical Baby*
3. *Dancing Deb* on revolving music stand

Girl Dolls Dressed Like Boys (cut off wig)
1. Arranbee: *Nancy Lee*
2. Mary Hoyer

6in (15.2cm) to 8in (20.3cm) *Ginny*-Type Dolls
Legs and Walker Mechanisms

Straight Leg Walkers
1. A & H: *Gigi*
2. Active: *Mindy*
3. Alexander: *Alexander kins, Wendy-kins*
4. Amanda Jane: England
5. Cosmopolitan: *Ginger* (early)
6. Doll Bodies: *Mary Lou*
7. Fortune: *Pam*
8. Hollywood: *Little Red*
9. Nancy Ann: *Muffie, Lori Ann*
10. Ontario Plastics: *Paula Sue,* Canada
11. Pedigree: *Shelly Ann,* England
12. Plastic Molded Arts: *Vicki, Petite Cherie, Joan, Joannie*
13. Richwood: *Sandra Sue*
14. Roberta: walker
15. Roddy: Made in England
16. Uneeda: *Janie*
17. Unique: *Vicki*
18. Virga; *Lucy,* Schiaparelli, *Go Go*
19. Vogue: *Ginny*

Non-walkers
1. Roberta: *Jeanie*
2. Doll Bodies
3. Vogue: *Ginny*

Hip Joint Walker
1. A & H: *Gigi*
2. PMA: *Petite Cheri*
3. Roberta 8½" (21.6cm)
4. Vogue: *Ginny*

Jointed Knees
1. A & H: *Gigi*
2. Alexander: *Alexanderkins, Wendy-kins, Quizkin*
3. Cosmopolitan: *Ginger* (later)
4. Nancy Ann
5. Roberta: walker
6. Vogue: *Ginny*

No Toe Detail
1. Uneeda: girl and boy

Molded Shoes
1. Doll Bodies: girl
2. Fortune: *Pam*
3. PMA: *Vicki*
4. Roberta: *Jeannie*
5. Virga: *Lucy*

Painted on Shoes - No Indication of Toes
1. A & H: *Gigi* (early)

Molded Unjointed Ballerina Feet
1. Fortune: *Pam*

WALKING DOLLS WHOSE HEADS TURN
COMPANIES

During the 1950s most walking dolls had a head turning mechanism. The following companies made these dolls.

1. A & H
2. Advance
3. Alexander
4. American Character
5. Arranbee
6. Beehler Arts
7. Belle
8. Cosmopolitan
9. Eegee
10. Effanbee
11. Fortune
12. G. H. & E. Freydberg
13. Horsman
14. Ideal
15. Imperial
16. Mollye
17. Nancy Ann
18. Natural Doll Co.
19. Plastic Molded Arts
20. Roberta
21. Roddy
22. Sayco
23. Star
24. Togs and Dolls
25. Uneeda
26. Valentine
27. Virga
28. Vogue

WALKING DOLLS WHOSE HEADS DO NOT TURN
COMPANIES

1. Arranbee
2. Eegee
3. Richwood
4. Roberta

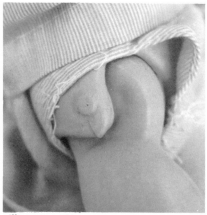

Illustration 629.

Illustration 631.

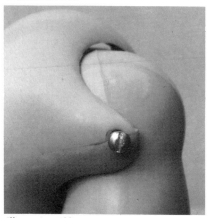

Illustration 630.

PIN JOINTED WALKING DOLLS

An excellent way to start to identify pin jointed walking dolls is through the pin itself. Repair to the mechanism will sometimes hamper the identification. Usually repair can be readily detected.

A. Painted, countersunk screw-type pin. Most Horsman dolls. A few Sayco dolls
    SEE: *Illustration 629.*

B. Unpainted screw. Most Ideal dolls. A few Imperial dolls.
    SEE: *Illustration 630.*

C. Unpainted rivet or painted rivet.
    Most Eegee dolls
    Most Imperial dolls
    Most Made in U.S.A. dolls
    Most Sayco dolls
    Most Valentine dolls
    SEE: *Illustration 631.*

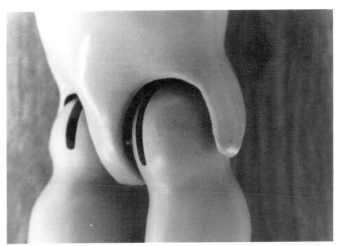

Illustration 632.

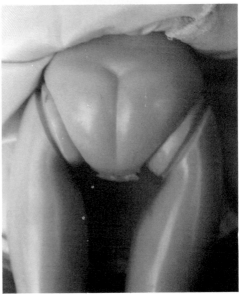

Illustration 633.

D.   Hidden pin. Usually these are found on the smaller or on the less expensive dolls.
   SEE: *Illustration 632.*

UNUSUAL FEATURE
   Some walking dolls have a peculiar molded leg with a ridge at the hip joint. Many of these dolls are unmarked. This doll is a Valentine doll, but the leg has been seen on other dolls such as a Mollye Circle X.
   MARKS: "11VW Made in U.S.A., Pat. Pending"
   SEE: *Illustration 633.*

WIGS AND HAIR

Swept Back Hairdo
1. Alexander
2. Arranbee
3. Ballerinas

Roll Bangs
1. Horsman
2. Ideal
3. Paris Walking doll
4. Unmarked *Saucy Walker* types

Plastic or Rubber Skull Cap for Rooted Hair
1. Alexander: *Binnie Walker*
2. American Char acter: *Sweet Sue, Betsy McCall, Tiny Tears*
3. Arranbee: *Taffy*

Caracul Fur Wig
1. American Character: *Tiny Tears*
2. Effanbee: *Patsy Babyette, Dy-Dee Baby*
3. Ideal: *Baby Gurglee*
4. Imperial: *Baby Linda* and others
5. Terri Lee: *Jerri, Tiny Jerri, Benji.* black *Terri*

Lambswool Wig
1. Terri Lee: *Connie Lynn, Jerri, Tiny Jerri*
2. Vogue: *Ginny*

Fur Wig
1. Imperial: girl, baby

Leather Wig
1. Paradise Walking Doll

Boys Flocked Hair
1. A & H: *Marcie*
2. Nancy Ann: *Lori Ann*
3. Plastic Molded Arts

Wind-up Hair
1. Arranbee: *Judy*

Hole in Molded Hair for Ribbon
1. Arranbee: *Peachy*

Hair Barrette - often seen on Alexander dolls.
  SEE: *Illustration 634.*

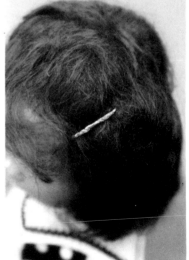

Illustration 634.

Bibliography

Books

Anderton, Johana Gast. *Twentieth Century Dolls from Bisque to Vinyl.* North Kansas City, Missouri: The Trojan Press, 1971.

_____. *More Twentieth Century Dolls from Bisque to Vinyl.* North Kansas City, Missouri: Athena Publishing Co., 1974.

_____. *More Twentieth Century Dolls. Vol. 1. A-H.* Des Moines, Iowa: Wallace-Homestead Book Co., 1981.

_____. *More Twentieth Century Dolls. Vol. 1. I-Z.* Des Moines, Iowa: Wallace-Homestead Book Co., 1981.

Antique Trader Weekly's Book of Collectible Dolls. Kyle D. Husfloen, ed. Dubuque, Iowa: Babka Publishing Co., 1976.

Axe, John. *Effanbee: A Collector's Encyclopedia.* Cumberland, Maryland: Hobby House Press, Inc., 1983.

_____. *The Encyclopedia of Celebrity Dolls.* Cumberland, Maryland: Hobby House Press, Inc., 1983.

Coleman, Dorothy S. *Lenci Dolls.* Riverdale, Maryland: Hobby House Press, 1977.

Cooper, Marlowe. *Doll Home Library Series, The First. Vol. 12. A Potpourri of Collectible Dolls.* 1973.

_____. *Doll Home Library Series, The Third. Vol. 14, A Potpourri of Collectible Dolls.* 1973.

Ellenburg, M. Kelly. *Effanbee, The Dolls with the Golden Heart.* North Kansas City, Missouri: The Trojan Press, 1973.

Foulke, Jan. *Treasury of Madame Alexander Dolls.* Riverdale, Maryland: Hobby House Press, 1979.

Freeman, Ruth S. *Cavalcade of Dolls, A Basic Source Book for Collectors.* Watkins Glen, New York: Century House Publishing Co., 1978.

Hoyer, Mary. *Mary Hoyer and Her Dolls.* Cumberland, Maryland: Hobby House Press, Inc., 1982.

Miller, Marjorie A. *Nancy Ann Storybook Dolls.* Cumberland, Maryland: Hobby House Press, 1980.

Niswonger, Jeanne Du Chateau. *That Doll Ginny.* Kissimmee, Florida: Cody Publications, 1983.

Smith, Patricia R. *Effanbee Dolls that Touch Your Heart.* Paducah, Kentucky: Collector Books, 1983.

_____. *Madame Alexander Collector's Dolls, Vol. 1 & 2.* Paducah, Kentucky: Collector Books,

_____. *Modern Collector's Dolls.* Paducah, Kentucky: Collector Books, 1973.

_____. *Modern Collector's Dolls. Second Series.* Paducah, Kentucky: Collector Books, 1975.

_____. *Modern Collector's Dolls. Third Series.* Paducah, Kentucky: Collector Books, 1976.

_____. *Modern Collector's Dolls. Fourth Series.* Paducah, Kentucky: Collector Books, 1979.

Uhl, Marjorie V. Sturges. *Madame Alexander Dolls on Review.* Dallas, Texas: Taylor Publishing Co., 1981.

_____. *Madame Alexander's Ladies of Fashion.* Paducah, Kentucky: Collector Books, 1979.

_____. *Madame Alexander Dolls are Made With Love.* Privately Printed. 1983.

Magazines

Bambini
Celebrity Doll Journal
Doll Castle News
Doll Reader®
Doll World
Dolls
McCall's Needlework & Crafts
Spinning Wheel

Price Guides

Foulke, Jan. *2nd Blue Book of Dolls and Values.*™ Riverdale, Maryland: Hobby House Press, 1976.

_____. *3rd Blue Book of Dolls and Values.*™ Riverdale, Maryland: Hobby House Press, 1978.

_____. *4th Blue Book of Dolls and Values.*™ Cumberland, Maryland: Hobby House Press, 1980.

_____. *5th Blue Book of Dolls and Values.*™ Cumberland, Maryland: Hobby House Press, 1982.

Glassmire, Carol Gast. *Price Guide to the Twentieth Century Dolls Series.* Des Moines, Iowa: Wallace-Homestead Book Co., 1981.

Herron, R. Lane. *Herron's Price Guide to Dolls and Paper Dolls.* Des Moines, Iowa: Wallace-Homestead Book Co., 1982.

Miller, Robert W. *Wallace-Homestead Price Guide to Dolls.* Des Moines, Iowa: Wallace-Homestead Book Co., 1982-1983.

The Official Price Guide to Dolls. Hudgeons, Thomas E., III., ed. Orlando, Florida: The House of Collectibles, Inc., 1983.

Smith, Patricia R. *Doll Values Antique to Modern. First Series.* Paducah, Kentucky: Collector Books., 1979.

_____. *Doll Values Antique to Modern. Second Series.* Paducah, Kentucky: Collector Books, 1980.

_____. *Doll Values Antique to Modern. Third Series.* Paducah, Kentucky: Collector Books, 1983.

_____. *Price Guide for Madame Alexander's Dolls. Number 9.* Paducah, Kentucky: Collector Books, 1983.

The Standard Modern Doll Identification and Value Guide. Paducah, Kentucky: Collector Books, 1979.

INDEX

BIOGRAPHY

From the time she was a little girl, Pam Judd has loved and collected dolls. Her mother, Polly, sewed for them, especially at Christmas. The family Christmas tree was decorated with foreign dolls brought from many lands by relatives and friends.

Later both Polly and Pam traveled to many lands, and the souvenirs always seemed to be dolls.

Gradually this interest turned to all types of doll collecting. A chance purchase at a local Goodwill store led to an interest in the beautiful hard plastic dolls.

Both authors are teachers and researchers who enjoy connecting the dolls with the history, culture, and costumes of the period of their manufacture. The beautiful dolls in this book, with their wonderful costumes, belong to the "Fabulous Fifties."